SO-BVR-185

SPALDING.

Baseball Trivia

SO YOU THINK YOU KNOW BASEBALL?

Property of:
Fort Morgan Public Library
Fort Morgan, Colorado

BOB ALLEY

MASTERS PRESS

A Division of Howard W. Sams & Co.

Masters Press (A Division of Howard W. Sams & Co.)
2647 Waterfront Pkwy. E. Drive, Suite 300
Indianapolis, IN 46214

© Robert S. Alley

All rights reserved. Published 1994.

Printed in the United States of America.

No part of this publication may be reproduced, stored in a retrieval system, or transmitted, in any form or by any means, electronic, mechanical, photocopying, or otherwise, without the prior permission of Masters Press.

Library of Congress Cataloging-in-Publication Data
   Alley, Robert S., 1932-

      Baseball trivia: so you think you know baseball? / Bob Alley.
          p. cm. -- (Spalding sports library)
      Includes bibliographical references.
      ISBN 0-940279-85-1
      1. Baseball--United States--Miscellanea. 2. Baseball--United States--History. 3. Baseball players--United States. I. Title. II. Series.
      GV876.3.A55   1993   94-43
      796.357'0973--dc20   CIP

Credits:
Cover design by Lynne Annette Clark
Edited by Jon Glesing

To my wonderful wife, Marjorie, my dearest friend who always supports all my endeavors, and to Ted, Yaz, Jimmy, Dom, Carlton, Mo, Bobby, Johnny, Rico, Boomer, Dwight, Luis, Looie and all the others who ever wore Red Sox.

Photo Credits

Masters Press would like to express its undying gratitude to the National Baseball Library & Archive and the major league teams for providing photographs for use in this text:

Atlanta Braves: photograph of David Justice by Bob Prior
Boston Red Sox: photograph of Jim Rice
Colorado Rockies: photograph of Andres Galarraga
Detroit Tigers: photograph of Cecil Fielder
Kansas City Royals: photograph of George Brett
Los Angeles Dodgers: photograph of Mike Piazza by Juan Ocampo
Milwaukee Brewers: photograph of Robin Yount
National Baseball Library & Archive (Cooperstown, N.Y.): photographs of Henry Aaron,
    Jackie Robinson, Charles Radbourne, and Ted Williams
New York Mets: photograph of Doc Gooden
San Francisco Giants: photographs of Barry Bonds and Willie Mays
Texas Rangers: photograph of Nolan Ryan

Table of Contents

Preface

Only a handful of people have had a greater impact on American life and culture than Alexander Cartwright. By establishing the first baseball team in 1845, the Knickerbocker Base Ball Club, this New York City bank teller triggered what would become organized baseball. Since then, millions of people have devoted themselves to baseball; admiring the best players and teams, and fascinated by the history and myths that surround the game.

Neither Cartwright nor Abner Doubleday (once believed to be baseball's inventor) created the game. American children have long been playing simplistic versions of baseball, a derivative of the English game "rounders." Cartwright, with a few rule modifications, transformed what had been viewed as a children's game during the mid-19th century into "The National Pastime."

Baseball has cast a spell on our culture. Artists place baseball images on canvas, writers create novels, historians record, and film makers document stories and images. Americans love baseball; from the start of spring training in late February to the World Series in October, we all share a knowledge of the game.

Cartwright's contribution is significant, because he was the first to divide the field into fair and foul territories. He also established the distance between bases at 90 feet and limited the number of players to nine. The game caught on with adults after Cartwright's modifications, and suddenly this "new" game became popular in the East. Cartwright extended baseball's popularity westward when, en route to California to seek his fortune during the 1849 gold rush, he taught the rules of the game to those he met along the way.

Some of baseball's magic has to do with how individual achievements and team successes don't diminish over time. For example, Henry Aaron and Roger Maris broke the immortal Babe Ruth's career home run record, but will "The Babe" ever be forgotten? Not likely. Similarly, shortstop Ozzie Smith has broken major league records set by Luis Aparacio. But older baseball enthusiasts aren't soon to forget the ease with which Aparacio and Nellie Fox turned the double play. The same goes for the awesome swings of Ted Williams or Joe DiMaggio; Carlton Fisk's 12th inning, game-winning home run in the 1975 World Series; or the 1969 New York Mets. Truly, baseball has provided us with seemingly countless memorable moments. They are what comprise baseball's ever-changing history. Fortunately, much has been written about baseball. This book is a tribute to all the writers who have recorded the facts, lore, legends, anecdotes and tales of baseball's greats, the-not-so great and everyone in between.

This book is a collection of exercises and anecdotes designated to entertain, teach and test the reader's memory and knowledge of "The National Pastime."

ON DECK IN THE AMERICAN LEAGUE

Can you answer these multiple choice questions about the American League? Eight correct answers makes you a major-leaguer; 11 vaults you to all-star status.

1. One of the best bunters in baseball was released from his team on Old Timer's Day in August of 1956. He was rehired as a play-by-play radio announcer the next season. In 1994, _____ was rehired by WPIX-Radio in New York City.

a. Phil Rizzuto
b. Andy Carey
c. Bobby Morgan

2. Who hit .390 in 1980, the highest since Ted Williams'.406 batting average in 1941?

a. George Brett
b. Rod Carew
c. Wade Boggs

3. In 1968, who became the first pitcher to win at least 30 games in a season since Lefty Grove won 31 in 1931?

a. Mike Norris
b. Jim Palmer
c. Dennis McLain

4. Who was the first African-American to play in the American League?

a. Pumpsie Green
b. Larry Dolby
c. Satchel Paige

5. On August 20, 1992, what family made baseball history when a Seattle Mariner became part of the first three-generation family to play in the majors (grandfather, father and son)?

a. Milt, Pinky and Jerry May
b. Ray, Bob and Bret Boone

6. Outfielder Jay Buhner, who hits about 40 points higher in day games, was traded to Seattle on July 21, 1988 from what team?

a. New York Yankees
b. New York Mets
c. Baltimore Orioles

7. On August 19, 1951, Eddie Gaedel became the smallest player in major league history (3 feet, 7 inches) when he pinch-hit for the St. Louis Browns. What was his uniform number?

a. 1/8
b. 1
c. 99

8. Who was the only player to ever pinch-hit for Ted Williams?

a. Gene Stephens
b. Carroll Hardy
c. Carl Yastrzemski

9. Who were the only two brothers to win a batting title?

a. Jesus and Matty Alou
b. Lloyd and Paul Waner
c. Harry "The Hat" and Dixie Walker

10. What was the last major league baseball team to integrate its roster (12 years after the Dodgers)?

a. Detroit
b. Boston
c. Chicago

11. What rising baseball star was shot and killed in Indiana in a case of mistaken identity in 1978?

a. Ed Delahanty
b. Ray Chapman
c. Lyman Bostock

12. What pitcher did the Cincinnati Reds get in exchange for trading Hall of Famer Frank Robinson to the Baltimore Orioles in 1961?

a. Dave McNally
b. Milt Pappas
c. Steve Barber

13. Which Boston Red Sox outfielder was the first major-leaguer to be named both Rookie of the Year and MVP in the same year?

a. Fred Lynn
b. Carl Yastrzemski
c. Ted Williams

14. On July 17, 1990, the Boston Red Sox hit into two triple plays in a single game. Who was their opponent?

a. Detroit
b. Minnesota
c. Oakland

Answers: *On Deck in the Amercian League*

1. a, Phil Rizzuto
2. a, George Brett
3. c, Dennis McLain. In addition to posting a 31-6 record and striking out a phenomenal 280 batters in 1968, McLain was named American League MVP and was a unanimous choice for the Cy Young Award. He won his second Cy Young Award a year later, but was suspended twice during the 1970 season by Commissioner Bowie Kuhn; April-June for gambling, and from September through the remainder of the season for carrying a gun. McLain was later traded to the Washington Senators (where Ted Williams was the manager) and then to Oakland. McLain's career was over by the end of the 1972 season. McLain spent much of the 1980s behind bars after being convicted on charges of drug possession, racketeering, extortion and gambling. He was released in 1989 and later worked as a musician in a Michigan bar and as host of a radio talk show.
4. b, Larry Doby
5. b, Ray, Bob and Bret Boone
6. a, Yankees
7. a, 1/8. Most baseball fans know the story of Eddie Gaedel, the midget who pinch-hit for the St. Louis Browns. The Browns were playing a doubleheader as part of the 50-year anniversary of the American League. Between games, Browns owner Bill Veeck, who was known for his outrageous promotional stunts, had a seven-foot hollow

birthday cake delivered to home plate. Inside was Gaedel. He popped out of the cake donning the number 1/8 on his back and a major league contract in his pocket. Gaedel pinch-hit in the bottom of the first inning of the second game. Legend has it Veeck threatened to shoot Gaedel if he swung at a pitch. Gaedel walked on four pitches and earned $100 for his appearance. Rookie Frank Saucier was the player Gaedel replaced. Stories circulated that Saucier, who was playing in his first major league game, was so incensed for being benched in place of a midget that he quit the team and never played the game again. Saucier may hold the record of the shortest major league career; half of one inning.

8. b, Caroll Hardy. During Hardy's major league career he totaled only 17 HRs, 113 RBI and a .225 lifetime batting average. He did, however, pinch-hit for the great Ted Williams after Williams fouled a pitch off his foot and was unable to continue his at bat. Hardy, like many good athletes, participated in two sports. He was a defensive back with the San Francisco 49ers in 1955.

9. c, Harry Walker. Walker was nicknamed "The Hat" because of his tendency to tug or adjust his cap after every pitch when batting. Over the course of a season he wore out as many as two-dozen caps. It was Walker who hit the memorable ground ball to Boston shortstop Johnny Pesky during the eighth inning of Game 7 of the 1946 World Series. Pesky hesitated on the play and his late throw to the plate allowed Enos Slaughter to score the winning run from third base. Walker's brother, Dixie, played nearly eight seasons in the American League before being traded to the Brooklyn Dodgers where he became known as "The People's Choice."

10. b, Boston
11. c, Lyman Bostock
12. b, Milt Pappas
13. a, Fred Lynn
14. b, Minnesota

3

ON DECK IN THE NATIONAL LEAGUE

Can you answer these multiple choice questions about the National League? Nine correct answers makes you a major-leaguer; 12 vaults you to all-star status.

1. Who was the New York Mets' first third baseman?

a. Cliff Cook
b. Charlie Neal
c. Don Zimmer

2. Who was the highest paid National League pitcher in 1993 ($5.6 million per year for three years)?

a. Bret Saberhagen
b. Greg Maddux
c. Doug Drabek

3. Which of the following applies to extra inning night games in the National League?

a. An inning may not begin after midnight
b. An inning may not begin after 1 a.m.
c. The National League has no rule or policy regarding late games

4. Two-time National League MVP Dale Murphy retired in 1993. He was hitting only .143 with no home runs at the time. With what team did Murphy end his career?

a. Atlanta
b. Philadelphia
c. Colorado

5. What team set the major league record of 23 consecutive losses in 1961?

a. Philadelphia
b. Chicago
c. New York

6. On June 27, 1993, New York's Anthony Young was the pitcher of record in a 5-2 loss to San Francisco. It was his 24th consecutive loss, a new major league record. Whose record did he break?

a. Cliff Curtis
b. John Curtis
c. Charles "Chief" Bender

7. Who broke the record for consecutive scoreless innings pitched in 1988 (58)?

a. Fernando Valenzuela
b. Orel Hershiser
c. Rick Sutcliffe

8. Referring to Question 7: Whose 20-year-old record did he break?

a. Sandy Koufax
b. Don Drysdale
c. Ron Perranowski

9. Who set the National League record for consecutive errorless games by a catcher in 1971 (138)?

a. Jerry Grote
b. Manny Sanguillen
c. Johnny Edwards

10. On June 15, 1993, Cubs relief pitcher Randy Myers gained his 20th save and became only the second pitcher to record 20 or more saves with four different teams. Who was the first to accomplish the feat?

a. Goose Gossage
b. Darold Knowles
c. Mike Marshall

11. Pete Rose hit only one grand slam home run during his career. Who threw the pitch?

a. Tommy Lasorda
b. Dallas Green
c. Nolan Ryan

12. After hitting his 100th career home run, what Met celebrated by circling the bases backward?

a. Jim Piersall
b. Frank Thomas
c. Cleon Jones

13. Who holds the National League single season record of 56 home runs?

a. Bob Elliott
b. Stan Musial
c. Hack Wilson

14. With what team did Babe Ruth end his career?

a. New York Giants
b. Boston Bees
c. Chicago Cubs

15. What National League team did "The Babe" coach?

a. Brooklyn Dodgers
b. Philadelphia Phillies
c. St. Louis Cardinals

Answers: *On Deck in the National League*

1. c, Don Zimmer. Zimmer played in the major leagues from 1954-65 and has been a manager or coach ever since. The expansion Mets drafted Zimmer from the Chicago Cubs and he became their first in a long list of third basemen. He played second base, third, shortstop and catcher during his career which included stints with the Dodgers, Cubs, Mets, Reds and Washington Senators.

   Another Zimmer, Charles "Chief" Zimmer (no relation to Don), is notable because in 1887 he became the first catcher to crouch directly behind the batter on every pitch to help ease the sting of catching without a glove. Considered the best defensive catcher of his time (he consistently led the National League in putouts, assists and double plays) it didn't take long for other catchers to begin mimicking Zimmer's style. Previously, catchers generally played further off the plate.

2. b, Greg Maddux
3. c, The National League has no rule or policy regarding late night games.
4. c, Colorado

5. a, Philadelphia
6. a, Cliff Curtis. Curtis' major league record 23-game losing streak stood for 82 years until Met pitcher Anthony Young broke it in June of 1993. Curtis came up with the Boston Braves in 1909. His career record was 28-61, with a 3.31 ERA. Curtis lasted five years in the majors, playing with the Cubs, Phillies and Dodgers.

Another pitcher, John Curtis, was a left-handed pitching sensation at Smithtown High School on Long Island, N.Y. While still in high school Curtis was regarded as a "can't miss" pitching prospect by pro scouts. Rejecting lucrative offers, Curtis accepted a scholarship to Clemson University where he threw three no-hitters as a freshman, and in the 1967 Pan American Games became the first U.S. pitcher to defeat a Cuban baseball team. Curtis eventually signed with the Boston Red Sox, and in his 1970 rookie year went 11-8. During his 15-year major league career Curtis pitched for the Cardinals, Giants, Padres and Angels in long and short relief roles, and finished 89-97 with a 3.96 ERA.

Charles "Chief" Bender became the first American Indian elected to the Baseball Hall of Fame. He was born in Minnesota in 1883. His mother was a Chippewa and his father a German settler. Bender grew up on an Indian reservation and later attended the Carlisle Indian School in Pennsylvania. In 1903 he came up with Connie Mack's Philadelphia Athletics where he played until 1914. In 1915 Bender "jumped" to Baltimore in the so-called "outlaw" Federal League. In 1916 he signed with the Phillies where he played two more seasons before retiring. Bender did it all, playing virtually every position and pinch hitting. He was 210-127 lifetime with a 2.46 ERA as a pitcher. He was proud to be an Indian but always signed autographs "Charley Bender."

7. b, Orel Hershiser
8. b, Don Drysdale
9. c, Johnny Edwards
10. a, Goose Gossage
11. b, Dallas Green
12. a, Jimmy Piersall
13. c, Hack Wilson
14. b, Boston Bees
15. a, Brooklyn Dodgers

THEY CALL ME...

Can you match the names with their appropriate nicknames? Six correct answers makes you a major leaguer; eight vaults you to all-star status.

AMERCIAN LEAGUE

1. _____ Puff
2. _____ Hawk
3. _____ The Georgia Peach
4. _____ The Commerce Comet
5. _____ Mr. October
6. _____ The Little Professor
7. _____ Superjew
8. _____ Psycho
9. _____ Gumby
10. _____ Pudge

CHOICES

a. Steve Lyons
b. Carlton Fisk
c. Mickey Mantle
d. Reggie Jackson
e. Graig Nettles
f. Dom DiMaggio
g. Jim Gantner
h. Ken Harrelson
i. Mike Epstein
j. Ty Cobb

NATIONAL LEAGUE

1. _____ Charlie Hustle
2. _____ Pee Wee
3. _____ The Natural
4. _____ Nails
5. _____ The Flying Dutchman
6. _____ The Big Cat
7. _____ The Donora Greyhound
8. _____ The Toy Cannon
9. _____ Rajah
10. _____ The Reading Rifle

a. Stan Musial
b. Carl Furillo
c. Jimmy Wynn
d. Honus Wagner
e. Lenny Dykstra
f. Rogers Hornsby
g. Pete Rose
h. Harold Henry Reese
i. Will Clark
j. Andres Galarraga

Andres Galarraga, also known as The Big Cat, batted .370 as a member of the expansion Colorado Rockies in 1993.

Answers: They Call Me...

AMERICAN LEAGUE

1. e, Graig Nettles. In his book *"Balls"* (co-authored with Peter Golenbock), Nettles wrote that in 1977 Yankee Manager Billy Martin wanted to use Reggie Jackson as a designated hitter. According to Nettles, "He (Jackson) was too much of a liability out there in the field...his skills were not as good as what we had on the bench." Nettles later wrote that Jackson's three home runs in the final game of the 1977 World Series against the Dodgers "was probably the greatest single-game performance by a player I've ever seen. It was amazing."
2. h, Ken Harrelson
3. j, Ty Cobb
4. c, Mickey Mantle
5. d, Reggie Jackson
6. f, Dom DiMaggio
7. i, Mike Epstein. Epstein played first base for the Orioles, Senators, Athletics, Rangers and Angels between 1966 and 1974. Lifetime he hit .244 with 130 HRs and 380 RBI. Epstein was nicknamed "Superjew" by minor league manager Rocky Bridges when *The Sporting News* named Epstein Minor League Player of the Year and the International League MVP in 1966. Unfortunately his major league career was marred by frequent strikeouts and poor defense. His best year was 1968 when he hit .278 with 30 HRs for the Senators. Some might be offended with the nickname, but Epstein bore it proudly.
8. a, Steve Lyons. Lyons was drafted as an infielder by Boston in the first round of the 1981 draft. He came up in 1985 as a rookie and played over 80 games in center field. Fans soon appreciated his hustle and recklessness, which earned him the nickname "Psycho." In 1986 Lyons was traded to the White Sox for Hall of Famer Tom Seaver. Lyons returned to Boston in 1993.
9. g, Jim Gantner
10. b, Carlton Fisk

NATIONAL LEAGUE

1. g, Pete Rose
2. h, Harold Henry Reese
3. i, Will Clark and Lenny Dykstra each hit home runs in their first major league at bat. Clark's was against baseball's all-time strikeout leader Nolan Ryan. "The Natural" shares the San Francisco team record of driving in runs in nine consecutive games with Willie Mays, Willie McCovey and Orlando Cepeda.
4. e, Lenny Dykstra. The New York media nicknamed Mets' lead off and No. 2 hitters Dykstra and Wally Backman "Partners in Grime" because of their hard-nosed, aggressive style of play.
5. d, Honus Wagner
6. j, Andres Galarraga
7. a, Stan Musial
8. c, Jimmy Wynn. Wynn was Houston's first slugging star. Before playing for the Dodgers, Braves, Yankees and Brewers, Wynn spent 11 seasons with the Astros, setting club records in almost every offensive category. "The Toy Cannon's" career nearly ended in December of 1970 when he was stabbed in the abdomen during an argument with his wife. He recovered, but never consistently returned to top form. The exception was in 1974 when the Dodger outfielder hit 32 HRs and was named Comeback Player of the Year.
9. f, Rogers Hornsby. Hornsby, considered by many as baseball's greatest right-handed hitter, had a lifetime .358 batting average. No modern player has hit higher than his .424 average in 1924. "Rajah's" 1929 season was good and bad. The up side was his .380 batting average, which included 39 HRs, 149 RBI and 156 runs scored. He was named MVP and led the Cubs to the pennant. The down side was the $100,000 he reportedly lost during that year's stock market crash.
10. b, Carl Furillo

THE "A" TEAM

Identify the individual whose last name begins with "A" that best fits the descriptions given. Seven correct answers makes you a major-leaguer; nine vaults you to all-star status.

a. Walter Alston

b. Joe Azcue

c. Luke Appling

d. Bernie Allen

e. Richie Ashburn

f. Grover Cleveland Alexander

g. Sandy Amoros

h. Joe Adcock

i. Tommy Agee

j. Willie Aikens

k. Luis Aparicio

1. This pitcher played with the Phillies in 1911 and was voted into the Baseball Hall of Fame in 1938. He posted a 373-208 career record with a 2.56 ERA. He and Christy Mathewson share the National League record for wins.

_____

2. This catcher, nicknamed "The Immortal," started his career with the Reds in 1960 and played with the Athletics, Indians, Red Sox, Angels and Brewers. In 1968 he batted .280 and was named an All-Star. He held out for the entire 1971 season and ended his career a year later with the Brewers.

_____

3. This first baseman started his career with the Reds in 1950, platooning with Ted Kluskewski, but made his mark with the Milwaukee Braves after being traded in 1953. On July 31, 1954, against the Dodgers, he hit four home runs and a double in one game, setting the single-game total base record (18). He played in two World Series with the Braves (1957-58) and hit 336 HRs and totaled 1,122 RBI.

_____

4. This second baseman had his best major league season as a rookie with the Twins in 1962 when he hit .269 with 12 HRs. After five seasons with the Twins, he played for the Senators and Yankees. An all-around athlete, he played quarterback at Purdue University.

_____

5. This third baseman, nicknamed "Old Aches and Pains," was one of the White Sox's all-time great infielders. Also occasionally playing shortstop, he had a lifetime batting average of .310 and over 1,300 walks.

_____

6. Most baseball fans won't have any trouble identifying this Hall of Fame shortstop. He was the 1956 Rookie of the Year as a member of the Chicago White Sox and later played with the Orioles and Red Sox, winning nine Gold Gloves during his career. His greatest seasons were in Chicago, playing next to second baseman Nellie Fox.

———————————

7. During Game 7 of the 1955 World Series, this part-time Brooklyn Dodger outfielder assured himself of a place in baseball history when he made what many believe the most outstanding defensive play in Series history. Playing in Yankee Stadium, he robbed Yogi Berra of a hit with two men on base by grabbing an opposite field line drive. Many believe that catch made the difference in the outcome of the Series.

———————————

8. This outfielder, who spent portions of his career with the Indians, White Sox, Mets, Astros and Cardinals, is best remembered as the center fielder/lead off hitter for the 1969 World Champion Mets. He slugged a career high 26 HRs that season.

———————————

9. This slick fielding outfielder finished his career as a member of the expansion New York Mets. He started with the Phillies in 1948 and returned to Philadelphia as a sportscaster after retiring from baseball. During his 15-year career he hit over .300 in nine seasons, winning two batting titles. He was an all-star in his first and last seasons. He was the first Met to be named to an All-Star team.

———————————

10. In 1980 this designated hitter/first baseman became the first player to have two multiple home run games in World Series history. He did it as a member of the Kansas City Royals. He was a regular first baseman with the Royals until his drug history surfaced. The Royals suspended him and eventually traded him to Toronto, where he finished his career as its designated hitter.

———————————

11. This former Dodger manager played in only one major league game – as a St. Louis Cardinal, and struck out during his only at bat. As a manager, however, he posted a .558 winning percentage and his teams won the National League pennant seven times (1955-56, 1959, 1963, 1965-66 and 1974). His record as the winning manager in seven-of-eight All-Star Games still stands.

———————————

Answers: The "A" Team

1. f, Grover Cleveland Alexander. Former sports announcer and United States President Ronald Reagan played the role of Grover Cleveland Alexander in the movie *"The Winning Team."* Despite the problems Alexander had as an epileptic and alcoholic, his won/loss record was outstanding. It was believed that he often pitched while drunk or suffering from a hangover. In his 1911 rookie year Alexander pitched 367 innings, winning 28 games, including seven shutouts (four in a row). He retired at age 40 after winning his 373rd game, passing Christy Mathewson on the National League's all-time wins list. It was later discovered that Mathewson was not credited with an additional win, which meant Mathewson and Alexander now share the National

record for victories. In addition, Alexander's best contract was when he was 40 in 1927. He won 21 games that year and was paid $17,500. During his career Alexander pitched for the Phillies, Cubs and Cardinals.

2. b, Joe Azcue
3. h, Joe Adcock
4. d, Bernie Allen
5. c, Luke Appling. "Old Aches and Pains" was so nicknamed because of his frequent ailments, some believed to be imaginary. Ailments or not, Appling could hit. His best season was in 1936, when he hit .388 and became the first White Sox player to win the batting title. He won it again in 1943 at age 35. He hit over .300 15 times during his 20-year career, spent entirely in Chicago. Appling began his career playing shortstop but finished at third base. He was once denied two free passes for a game at New York. To retaliate, he intentionally hit 25 consecutive foul balls during batting practice before Yankee officials granted his request. Baseballs cost a lot more than passes to a game in those days.
6. k, Luis Aparicio. How much would a shortstop like Aparicio be worth today? Not only was Aparicio a nine-time Gold Glove winner, but he also led the American League in stolen bases a record nine times. During his career, Aparicio established records for games played by a shortstop, assists and putouts on double plays, and set an all-time single season best with a .983 fielding percentage.
7. g, Sandy Amoros

8. i, Tommy Agee. During Agee's 11-year career he was the 1966 Rookie of the Year as a member of the White Sox, was twice named to the All-Star Team and was a Gold Glove recipient. However, he is remembered most for his play during the third game of the 1969 World Series against Baltimore, where he led off the first inning with a home run. In the third, and the Mets ahead 3-0, Agee made a sensational catch, bouncing off the center field wall and preventing two runs from scoring. Three innings later he snared a line drive by Paul Blair with the bases loaded. It was a ball few Shea Stadium fans thought he could reach, let alone catch.
9. e, Richie Ashburn. Three early Mets were Ashburn, Al Jackson and "Marvelous" Marv Throneberry. In 1962, New York won just 62 games. In one game, Jackson pitched 15 innings of three-hit baseball but lost because of two errors by Throneberry, the first baseman. Later that season Ashburn congratulated Throneberry on his birthday by saying "We were going to give you a cake, but we thought you'd drop it." On another occasion Throneberry hit a ball to the deepest part of the park, rounded first and second, and slid safely into third. He was called out, however, when the umpire ruled Throneberry failed to touch second base. When Manager Casey Stengel emerged from the dugout to argue the call his first base coach said, "Don't bother, Casey. He didn't touch first, either."
10. j, Willie Aikens
11. a, Walt Alston

MVP MIXUP

Can you match the names of the players with the team they played for when they were named MVP? Six correct answers makes you a major-leaguer; eight vaults you to all-star status.

AMERICAN LEAGUE

1. _____ Lefty Grove, pitcher
2. _____ Thurman Munson, catcher
3. _____ Hank Greenberg, first base
4. _____ Nellie Fox, second base
5. _____ Harmon Killebrew, third
6. _____ Robin Yount, shortstop
7. _____ George Bell, outfield
8. _____ Jim Rice, outfield
9. _____ Jeff Burroughs, outfield

TEAMS

a. Detroit Tigers
b. Minnesota Twins
c. Chicago White Sox
d. Boston Red Sox
e. New York Yankees
f. Texas Rangers
g. Milwaukee Brewers
h. Philadelphia Athletics
i. Toronto Blue Jays

NATIONAL LEAGUE

1. _____ Don Newcombe, pitcher
2. _____ Bob O'Farrell, catcher
3. _____ Willie Stargel, first base
4. _____ Maury Wills, second base
5. _____ Mike Schmidt, third base
6. _____ Ernie Banks, shortstop
7. _____ George Foster, outfield
8. _____ Willie Mays, outfield
9. _____ Dale Murphy, outfield

a. Atlanta Braves
b. Los Angeles Dodgers
c. Cincinnati Reds
d. St. Louis Cardinals
e. Brooklyn Dodgers
f. Philadelphia Phillies
g. San Francisco Giants
h. Pittsburgh Pirates
i. Chicago Cubs

Answers: MVP Mixup
AMERICAN LEAGUE

1. h, Philadelphia Athletics (1931). Lefty Grove, a Hall of Famer, won 300 games while pitching nine seasons for Connie Mack's Philadelphia Athletics. Grove played another nine seasons with the Boston Red Sox. At one point, he led the American League in strikeouts seven consecutive seasons. Grove also had the league's lowest ERA nine times. In 1931 he won 31 games, including 16 in a row. Grove had a legendary temper and when riled would throw at anyone, including his teammates. Grove's Philadelphia teammates feared for their lives should they accidentally hit a ball back toward the mound when Grove threw batting practice because he would retaliate by throwing "at their pockets." Grove's teammates got the last laugh, however. They eventually made it a habit to intentionally hit Grove's last batting practice pitch at him knowing he would be unable to retaliate. About opposing hitters, Grove once said, "I'd hit them in the middle of the back or hit 'em in the foot, it didn't make any difference to me. But, I'd never throw at a man's head, never believed in it." Rather than sign autographs, Grove had a rubber stamp with a facsimile of his signature.

2. e, New York Yankees (1976). In 1970, Thurman Munson became the New York Yankees' starting catcher after playing less than 100 games in the minor leagues. He was almost sent back to the minors after getting off to a slow start. Manager Ralph Houk refused to give up on him, however, and Munson finished the year as the American League's Rookie of the Year.

3. a, Detroit Tigers (1935)
4. c, Chicago White Sox (1959)
5. b, Minnesota Twins (1969)
6. g, Milwaukee Brewers (1982). In 1974, Robin Yount began his career as an 18-year-old shortstop with the Milwaukee Brewers. Yount's 1982 season was his best and he was rewarded by being named the American League's MVP. He hit .331 with 29 HRs and 114 RBI that year. He also led the league in hits, doubles and assists by a shortstop. Early in his career, Yount considered giving up his baseball career to pursue fame and fortune as a professional golfer. Brewer fans are happy he continued in baseball and as of the conclusion of the 1993 season he led all active players with over 2,600 games played with the same organization.

7. i, Toronto Blue Jays (1987)

8. d, Boston Red Sox (1978). Looking back at recent major league history, Jim Rice certainly is one of baseball's more underrated players. He was last in a succession of three great Red Sox left fielders which included Ted Williams and Carl Yastrzemski. Rice's obscurity began as a rookie, playing alongside fellow neophyte Fred Lynn. Rice's impressive .300-plus batting average, 22 HRs, 102 RBI inaugural season was overshadowed by Lynn's Rookie of the Year performance. In addition, Rice broke his hand when he was hit by a pitch during the final week of the 1975 season, thus missing the World Series. That injury was just another incident in a series that became known as "Curse of the Bambino." Rice played over 2,000 games during his career, leading the league in home runs three times, twice in RBI, and was repeatedly named to the All-Star Team. During his 1978 MVP season Rice batted .315 with 213 hits, including 46 HRs, 15 triples, 400 total bases and a slugging percentage of .600. The low point of Rice's career was in 1989, his final season, when manager Joe Morgan sent infielder Spike Owen to pinch-hit for him. That "humiliation" resulted in a shoving match with Mor-

Early in his career Robin Yount considered giving up baseball to pursue fame and fortune as a professional golfer. Instead, he spent 20 years with the Milwaukee Brewers.

Jim Rice played over 2,000 games during his 16-year career with the Boston Red Sox, leading the American League in home runs three times, twice in RBI, and was repeatedly named to the All-Star Team. Among all Red Sox players only Ted Williams and Carl Yastrzemski had more home runs, RBI and total bases.

gan. Among all Red Sox players only Ted Williams and Carl Yastrzemski had more home runs, RBI and total bases.

9. f, Texas Rangers (1974)

NATIONAL LEAGUE

1. e, Brooklyn Dodgers. In 1956, Don Newcombe was named MVP after going 27-7 for the pennant winning Dodgers. He was 149-90 during his career, but never seemed to be able to put it all together during postseason play. He appeared in three Worlds Series and never won a game. He pitched a total of 22 innings in five appearances and gave up 21 earned runs. Despite this lack of success in the World Series, Newcombe was an excellent pitcher. He is commonly recognized as the first outstanding black pitcher to play in the majors.

2. d, St. Louis Cardinals (1926)

3. h, Pittsburgh Pirates (1980)

4. b, Los Angeles Dodgers (1962)

5. f, Philadelphia Phillies (1980, 1981, 1986)

6. i, Chicago Cubs (1958, 1959)

7. c, Cincinnati Reds (1977)

8. g, San Francisco Giants (1965). Willie Mays was actually named an MVP twice, first with the then-New York Giants in 1954 and again in 1965 with the San Francisco Giants. Mays is the only player to be an MVP for the same team but in different cities. The 11 years separating the honors is also a record among multiple MVP winners.

Frank "Wildfire" Schulte won the first National League MVP award in 1911. He hit .300 with 21 HRs, 30 doubles and 21 triples with the Cubs that year. He led the league with 121 RBI and also stole 23 bases. Schulte was the first to total more than 20 doubles, triples, home runs and stolen bases in a single season. In 1954, Mays became the second. Mays was indeed an inspirational player; so much so that he inspired two songs, both recorded in 1954. A group called The Treniers recorded "Say Hey, Willie", which included Mays on vocals. The second song was "The Amazing Willie Mays" by The King Odum Quartet.

Mays wasn't the only baseball hero to appear on a recording. Former Los Angeles Dodger shortstop and feared base stealer Maury Wills recorded "The Ballad of Maury Wills" in 1964. He once appeared in a Las Vegas nightclub singing the ballad, accompanying himself on his banjo. What a show that must have been.

There are a number of MVM (Most Valuable Musicians) in baseball lore. Charlie Pride, Roy Acuff, Jim Reeves and Conway Twitty all became major league country music performers after brief careers in minor league baseball.

9. a, Atlanta Braves (1982, 1983). Dale Murphy, who retired during the 1993 season, began his major league career with the Atlanta Braves in 1976. He originally signed as a catcher but surprisingly had trouble throwing the ball back to the pitcher. Murphy switched from catcher to first base, where he played until the Braves traded for Chris Chambliss at the end of the 1979 season. In 1980, Murphy moved to the outfield and soon proved to be a fine defensive outfielder as well as a potent offensive player. Murphy led his team to the pennant during his MVP seasons. He was a Gold Glove winner who twice led the league in slugging percentage and became the youngest player in National League history to win back-to-back MVP Awards.

Willie Mays is the only player to be the MVP for the same team but in different cities – the New York and San Francisco Giants.

ALL IN THE FAMILY

Can you answer these 19 questions about three present major league standouts whose fathers also played in the majors? The answers to questions 1-12 are found in the Box Score Comparison on the next page. Ten correct answers makes you a major-leaguer; 12 vaults you to all-star status.

Player:	a. Moise Alou	b. Ken Griffey, Jr.	c. Brian McRea
Team:	Montreal Expos	Seattle Mariners	Kansas City Royals
Father:	Filipe Alou	Ken Griffey	Hal McRea

1. Which son had the highest batting average in 1993?

2. Who had the most at bats?

3. Who scored the most runs?

4. Who had the fewest hits during the season?

5. Who had the most extra base hits (not including home runs)?

6. Who hit the most home runs?

7. Who hit the fewest home runs?

8. Who had the most RBI?

9. Who had the fewest RBI?

10. Who stole the most bases?

11. Who made the most errors?

12. Who made the fewest errors?

EXTRA CREDIT

13. Who was the last to arrive in the majors?

14. Who didn't play for a manager who was also his father in 1993?

15. Who was the first to play in the same organization at the same time as his father?

16. Which son and his father were the first father and son combination to play in the majors at the same time?

17. Who was signed as a shortstop?

18. Was Brian McRea's 1993 batting average higher or lower than his father's lifetime average?

19. Was Ken Griffey, Jr.'s 1993 average higher or lower than his father's lifetime average?

1993 Box Score Comparison

Player	AVG	AB	R	H	XBH	HR	RBI	S	E
a. Moise Alou	.286	482	70	138	35	18	85	17	4
b. Ken Griffey, Jr.	.308	574	111	177	40	45	109	16	3
c. Brian McRea	.285	620	78	177	37	12	69	23	7

Answers to questions 13-19:
13. a, Moise Alou; 14. b, Ken Griffey, Jr.; 15. c, Brian McRae; 16. b, Ken Griffey, Jr.; 17. c, Brian McRae; 18. Lower; 19. Higher

INFIELD PRACTICE

Can you answer these multiple choice questions about major league infielders? Seven correct answers makes you a major-leaguer; nine vaults you to all-star status.

1. Which of the following is generally considered to have been the best bunter in baseball history, leading the majors in sacrifice hits an unequalled four consecutive years?

a. Phil Rizzuto
b. Buddy Harrelson
c. Jackie Robinson
d. Johnny Pesky

2. Who is the only player to make an unassisted triple play in the World Series?

a. Gil McDougal
b. Bill Wambsgauss
c. Brooks Robinson
d. Wally Backman

3. Who, in 1990, set the major league record of 95 consecutive errorless games played by a shortstop?

a. Cal Ripkin
b. Kevin Elster
c. Ozzie Smith

4. On October 1, 1989, Ryne Sandberg of the Chicago Cubs set a new major league record of 90 consecutive errorless games by a second baseman. Whose record did he break?

a. Joe Gordon
b. Doug Flynn
c. Manny Trillo

5. Who holds the National League career record for being hit by a pitch (243)?

a. Ron Hunt
b. Davey Lopes
c. Red Schoendienst

6. Which of the following first basemen holds the single season record for having a perfect fielding percentage (1.000)?

a. Steve Garvey
b. Willie Montanez
c. Keith Hernandez
d. Don Mattingly

7. On May 31, 1992 Gary Carter caught his 2,000th game. Only two others have caught as many. Both are listed below. Who doesn't belong?

a. Bob Boone
b. Carlton Fisk
c. Yogi Berra

8. Which first baseman became known as "The Right-handed Babe Ruth?"

a. Jimmie Foxx
b. Johnny Mize
c. Bill Terry
d. Rudy York

9. Who was the only person to ever pinch-hit for Joe DiMaggio?

a. Jerry Coleman
b. Bobby Brown
c. Phil Rizzuto
d. Snuffy Stirnweiss

10. In 1992 Ozzie Smith was awarded his 13th Gold Glove Award, the most ever in the National League. How many of those were won in succession?

a. 4
b. 6
c. 9
d. 13

11. Who holds the record of 16 career Gold Gloves?

a. Lou Gehrig
b. Brooks Robinson
c. Bobby Doerr
d. Joe Morgan

12. Which catcher retired with a lifetime batting average of .320, the highest for the position?

a. Bill Dickey
b. Birdie Tebbetts
c. Mickey Cochrane
d. Carlton Fisk

Answers: Infield Practice

1. a, Phil Rizzuto
2. b, Bill Wambsgauss. It was during the 1920 Brooklyn/Cleveland World Series that Wambsgauss turned an unassisted triple play. It occurred during Game 5 with Dodgers on first and second. Clarence Mitchell hit the line drive that started the play. Wambsgauss caught the ball, stepped on second base and tagged the runner between first and second. Cleveland won the game 8-1 and the series 4-3 after losing the first three games.
3. a, Cal Ripkin
4. c, Manny Trillo
5. a, Ron Hunt
6. a, Steve Garvey
7. c, Yogi Berra
8. a, Jimmie Foxx was nicknamed "The Right-handed Babe Ruth" in 1932 when, as a member of the Boston Red Sox, he hit 58 home runs and had 175 RBI. A sore wrist during a portion of the season contributed to Foxx falling just short of Ruth's record 60-home run season. Another factor weighing against Foxx were large screens erected in two ballparks after Ruth's legendary season, making it more difficult to hit home runs. Foxx hit those screens eight times that season. Opposing pitchers learned to pitch around Foxx early that year. In one June game, he walked a record six consecutive times.
9. c, Phil Rizzuto. While broadcasting a New York Yankee game in 1992, Rizzuto told a story of how he became the only player to pinch-hit for the great Joe DiMaggio. It was late in the game and the Yankees were batting. DiMaggio wasn't due to bat right away in the inning so he went into the locker room to use the rest room. When his turn came around to hit, DiMaggio hadn't returned. Manager Joe McCarthy looked down the bench and called on Rizzuto, a rookie, to take DiMaggio's place.
10. c, 13
11. b, Brooks Robinson. Many consider Robinson the best ever at his position. In the 1970 Baltimore/Cincinnati World Series he batted .429, hit two home runs and made numerous spectacular defensive plays. Robinson was named the Series' MVP for that performance. He was held in such high regard that he was named the starting third baseman for the All-Star Game an astounding 15 seasons in a row, taking home Gold Glove trophies every year between 1960 and 1975. He was inducted into the Baseball Hall of Fame in 1983.
12. c, Birdie Tebbetts. Tebbetts was a good hitting catcher for the Tigers, Red Sox and Indians. His lifetime batting average was a respectable .270, but not in the same league as Mickey Cochrane's .320. Tebbetts' given name is George, but his teammates at Providence College nicknamed him "Birdie" because of his high pitched voice. During his major league career he had exactly 1,000 hits and went on to manage for 11 years. Prior to Tebbetts' first major league game he was accidentally hit in the mouth with a ball during infield practice. He went on to catch the entire game and hit a game-winning double. After the game Tebbetts' Detroit teammates discovered his mouth had been bleeding the entire game and he had been swallowing the blood. It took seven stitches in Tebbetts' lip to stop the bleeding.

WHO SAID IT?

Can you match the quotes with the person who said them? Nine correct answers makes you a major-leaguer; 11 vaults you to all-star status.

a. Reggie Jackson

b. Don Baylor

c. Babe Ruth

d. Pete Rose

e. Lou Gehrig

f. Ron Hunt

g. Ken Harrelson

h. Phil Rizzuto

i. Tug McGraw

j. Mel Allen

k. Connie Mack

l. Casey Stengel

m. Bill Lee

n. Yogi Berra

1. This former National League second baseman, who wasn't afraid of being hit by a pitch, said, "Some people give their bodies to science; I give mine to baseball."

_____

2. This relief pitcher inspired his New York Met teammates during the 1973 pennant race with the charge "You gotta believe."

_____

3. This owner/manager, searching for the positives after a fourth place finish, said "You don't have to give the players raises when they don't win."

_____

4. This player, best known for his time in Boston, admitted he used marijuana, but "only when sprinkled on cereal."

_____

5. This free agent signed by the Yankees described himself as "the straw that stirred the drink."

_____

6. This first baseman/outfielder played with the Kansas City Athletics until 1967 when, in a fit of anger, he was quoted as saying "(Owner) Charlie Finley is a menace to baseball." He was immediately released, but promptly signed with the Red Sox and received a hefty bonus.

_____

23

7. Who said, "I want to thank all you people for making Phil Rizzuto this night necessary," while being honored during a special night at the ballpark?

_____

8. Who shouts "Holy Cow!" whenever something good happens during a Yankees game?

_____

9. Who said, "It's great to be back in the Polar Grounds again with the New York Knickerbockers," when introduced as the manager of an expansion team?

_____

10. Who said, "I had a better year than he did," when informed his $80,000 annual salary was $5,000 more than President Hoover's?

_____

11. "Ouch" was all this person could say after being struck by a pitch for a record 244th time.

_____

12. This person frequently had the opportunity to say "That ball is going, going, gone!" during Yankees games.

_____

13. This player/manager said, "I would walk through hell in a gasoline suit to keep playing baseball."

_____

14. "Today I consider myself the luckiest man on the face of the earth," was what legendary Yankee's way of thanking the fans for their support when he addressed a Yankee Stadium crowd on July 4, 1939?

_____

Answers: Who Said It?

1. f, Ron Hunt
2. i, Tug McGraw
3. k, Connie Mack. Mack was the owner/manager of the Philadelphia Athletics for 50 years and retired in 1950 at age 88. He started managing in 1901 with 25 percent ownership of the team and gradually became sole owner. During his managerial career, Mack set records for wins (3,776), losses (4,025) and total games (7,878) - marks not likely to ever be surpassed. Unlike typical managers who wear uniforms in the dugout, Mack preferred to dress more like an owner. He wore a business suit for every game.
4. m, Bill Lee. Lee, who pitched for the Red Sox, was nicknamed "Spaceman," in part be-
cause he sometimes wrote "Earth" after his name when signing autographs. He was a favorite among the media and fans because he had a quick wit and wasn't afraid to say what was on his mind. An example occurred against Detroit. Tiger Al Kaline took ball four and as he trotted to first base Lee shouted from the mound, "Swing the bat! You're not a statue until you have pigeon (droppings) on your shoulders."
5. a, Reggie Jackson
6. g, Ken Harrelson
7. n, Yogi Berra
8. h, Phil Rizzuto
9. l, Casey Stengel
10. c, Babe Ruth. It was customary to see Ruth sitting at a table and playing cards to pass

the time on the train when the Yankees were on the road. It was also customary for Ruth to be accompanied by a bottle of whiskey, which he never shared with his teammates, as he played Hearts, his favorite card game.

11. b, Don Baylor
12. j, Mel Allen
13. d, Pete Rose
14. e, Lou Gehrig

THE BIG BOYS

Can you answer these multiple choice questions about home run hitters? Sixteen correct answers makes you a major-leaguer; 18 vaults you to all-star status.

1. What two New York Yankees combined to hit a record 115 home runs in a single season?

a. Joe DiMaggio/Charlie "King Kong" Keller
b. Babe Ruth/Lou Gehrig
c. Mickey Mantle/Roger Maris

2. Detroit's Cecil Fielder hit 51 home runs in 1990. Who was the last to hit at least 50 before Fielder?

a. Mickey Mantle
b. Johnny Bench
c. George Foster
d. Ted Williams

3. Who wrote the famous poem "The Mighty Casey?"

a. Ernest L. Thayer
b. Robert Louis Stevenson
c. Grantland Rice
d. Emily Dickinson

4. Who, in 1990, was the first player to earn $4 million a year?

a. Will Clark
b. Jose Canseco
c. Joe Carter

5. Willie Mays was the first to amass at least 2,000 base hits, 300 home runs and 300 stolen bases. Who, in 1990, became the second?

a. Andre Dawson
b. Dave Winfield
c. Dwight Evans

6. Who, in 1989, tied Lou Gehrig's American League record of four three-home run games in a career?

a. Robin Yount
b. Joe Carter
c. Jose Canseco

7. Who totaled a record 12 RBI in a single game on September 16, 1924?

a. George Sisler
b. Jim Bottomly
c. Babe Ruth

8. In what city did Babe Ruth start his professional baseball career?

a. Boston
b. Baltimore
c. Boise

9. Who hit his 100th home run during his 1,351st at bat, the quickest to reach that milestone in baseball history?

a. Ralph Kiner
b. Jimmie Foxx
c. Willie Mays

10. What Boston outfielder became the youngest player to win the home run title when he hit 32 in 1965?

a. Jackie Jensen, age 22
b. Ted Williams, age 21
c. Tony Conigliaro, age 20

11. Who hit an American League single season record five grand slam home runs in 1961, a record that stood until 1987?

a. Jim Gentile
b. Orlando Cepeda
c. Don Mincher

12. Who is the only MVP to hit 50 or more home runs in a season?

a. George Foster
b. Hank Aaron
c. Mickey Mantle

13. Who hit a record 49 home runs as a rookie?

a. Jose Canseco
b. Mark McGwire
c. Bobby Bonilla

14. Who was the first player to hit at least 30 home runs his first four years?

a. Frank Howard
b. Mark McGwire
c. Barry Bonds

15. What New York Yankee hit a record 61 home runs in a single season?

a. Babe Ruth
b. Mickey Mantle
c. Roger Maris

16. What Japanese baseball team did Cecil Fielder play for prior to joining the Detroit Tigers?

a. Hanshin Tigers
b. Tokyo Carp
c. Kintetsu Buffaloes

17. What New York Yankee holds the record for the most home runs in World Series competition (18)?

a. Mickey Mantle
b. Babe Ruth
c. Joe DiMaggio

18. Which home run hitter had the most career walks?

a. Ted Williams
b. Babe Ruth
c. Henry Aaron

19. Who holds the National League record of eight consecutive games with a home run?

a. Dale Long
b. Ernie Banks
c. Joe Torre

20. How many home runs did career leader Henry Aaron hit?

a. 714
b. 733
c. 755

21. Which home run hitter hit into the most double plays?

a. Henry Aaron
b. Babe Ruth
c. Harmon Killebrew

22. Two players share the record for hitting home runs in 32 different major league ballparks. Of the players listed, who doesn't belong?

a. Rusty Staub
b. Frank Robinson
c. Orlando Cepeda

23. What New York Yankee holds the single season record of six grand slam home runs?

a. Lou Gehrig
b. Don Mattingly
c. Tommy Henrich
d. Babe Ruth

Answers: The Big Boys

1. c, Mickey Mantle/Roger Maris. The 1961 Yankees won 109 games and hit a record 240 home runs. Maris and Mantle combined for 115 homers and 270 RBI. Maris broke Babe Ruth's single season record of 60 home runs with No. 61 that year (question 15) but needed the extended 162-game schedule (from 154 games). The Yankees went on to win their 19th championship despite Mantle and Maris playing poorly in the World Series. Mantle played in only two games be-

cause of sore legs. Maris, who batted only .105 for the series with a home run, was exhausted from the constant harassment by Ruth and Mantle fans, as well as the hounding media. The pressure to beat Ruth's record became so great that he started losing his hair. Detroit first baseman Norm Cash and the Tigers also had a good year in 1961. The Tigers won 101 games, ordinarily good enough to win the pennant. Cash totaled 41 HRs and 132 RBI, but his achievements were overshadowed by the Yankees' success and rumors that he used corked bats.

2. c, George Foster
3. a, Ernest L. Thayer
4. b, Jose Canseco
5. a, Andre Dawson
6. b, Joe Carter
7. b, Jim Bottomly
8. b, Baltimore
9. a, Ralph Kiner
10. c, Tony Conigliaro
11. a, Jim Gentile
12. c, Mickey Mantle
13. b, Mark McGwire
14. b, Mark McGwire
15. c, Roger Maris
16. a, Hanshin Tigers
17. a, Mickey Mantle
18. b, Babe Ruth
19. a, Dale Long
20. c, 755. At the conclusion of the 1973 season, Henry Aaron was one home run shy of Babe Ruth's career record of 714. Aaron received thousands of threatening letters that year from Ruth admirers who did not want to see the record broken. On one occasion the FBI suspected a plot to kidnap his daughter, Gaile, a student at Fisk University. Aaron received police protection when coming and going from the ballpark and registered in hotels under false names. Unfortunately, much of the hostility toward Aaron hinged on the fact an African-American was challenging Ruth's record. Regard-

Henry Aaron broke Babe Ruth's home run record with this swing on April 8, 1974. It was Aaron's 715th career home run. He retired in 1976 with 755.

less, Aaron went on to shatter Ruth's mark, finishing with 755 career home runs. Aaron's brother, Tommie, also played in the majors. They hold the record for the most home runs by a brother combination; Henry with 755 and Tommie with 13.

21. a; Henry Aaron
22. c; Orlando Cepeda
23. b; Don Mattingly

GRAB BAG

Can you answer these true/false questions? Fourteen correct answers makes you a major-leaguer; 16 vaults you to all-star status.

1. The Baltimore Orioles were sold for $173 million in 1993, more than $100 million more than the previous owner, Eli Jacobs, paid for the team.

2. The Orioles' new owners include novelist Tom Clancy, author of "The Hunt for Red October," and tennis player Pam Shriver.

3. During August of 1993, Scott Erickson pitched the first complete game of the season for the Minnesota Twins. Previously, the Twins had gone to the bullpen in 105 straight games, a major league record.

4. Tom Seaver faced Mickey Mantle only once and struck him out.

5. The 1881 New York Mets were the first professional major league baseball club in New York City.

6. Ted Williams was voted Manager of the Year while with the Washington Senators in 1969.

7. Sandy Amoros became a Brooklyn Dodger hero in Game 7 of the 1955 World Series when he made a spectacular catch off the bat of Billy Martin of the Yankees.

8. Mickey Mantle has more postseason home runs than Reggie Jackson.

9. Reggie Jackson was the 29th pick of the Kansas City Athletics in 1966 and received a $850 bonus when he signed his contract.

10. Stan Musial had more extra base hits than Babe Ruth.

11. Pitcher Tom Seaver won more than 300 games.

12. During July of 1993, the Colorado Rockies set a night game attendance record when 71,784 fans attended a game.

13. The maximum bat length allowed in the major leagues is 48 inches.

14. Dave Kingman hit more grand slam home runs than Joe DiMaggio.

15. Babe Ruth hit more grand slam home runs than Hank Aaron.

16. Ty Cobb was never named a Most Valuable Player.

17. Ben Chapman, who played in the New York Yankee outfield alongside Babe Ruth, made history as the first batter in the first All-Star Game.

18. The first All-Star Game was played at Chicago's Comiskey Park in 1933.

19. Dave Stewart and Fernando Valenzuela made baseball history when they each threw no-hitters on the same day in 1990.

20. Randy Johnson became the tallest pitcher in major league history to throw a no-hitter in 1990.

Ted Williams hit .406 in 1941, the highest batting average in baseball history.

Answers: Grab Bag

1. True. The $173 million paid for the Orioles was the highest price ever paid in the United States for a professional sports team. The previous record had been the $140 million paid for the Dallas Cowboys in 1989.
2. True
3. True
4. True, according to Seaver while talking with Phil Rizzuto during a Yankee game broadcast. If so, it would have occurred in an exhibition game.
5. True. The Brooklyn Athletics were already in existence but played outside New York City. Brooklyn was a separate city at the time.
6. True. The 1969 Washington Senators won 86 games, a 21-game improvement over the previous year and first-year manager Ted Williams was named Manager of the Year. He managed until 1972, retiring from the game following a 54-100 season. Williams may have had limited success as a manager but few can argue his legend as a hitter. In 1941, Williams entered the last day of the season with a .396 batting average. Boston Manager Joe Cronin wanted Williams to sit out the scheduled doubleheader, thinking Williams could round up the average to .400. Williams chose to play and tallied six hits, increasing his average to .406. Williams is the only person to seriously challenge his own mark, hitting .388 in 1957.
7. False. Sandy Amoros' remarkable catch was off the bat of Yogi Berra. The game was played in Yankee Stadium and the drama unfolded in the bottom of the sixth inning with the Dodgers leading 2-0. Dodger Manager Walter Alston moved left fielder Jim Gilliam to second base after pulling regular second baseman Don Zimmer for a pinch hitter in the top half of the inning. Gilliam was replaced in the outfield by Amoros off

the bench. Billy Martin opened the Yankees' half of the inning with a walk and Gil McDougald followed with a bunt single. Berra was up next with two runners on base and the outfield shaded toward right field. Berra ripped an opposite field line drive to left. After the game Amoros was quoted as saying, "I just run like hell" when asked about the play. Not only did Amoros make the catch, but he rifled the ball to Pee Wee Reese at shortstop, who doubled McDougald at first base. The Dodgers won the game 2-0 and the series 4-3. It was the Dodgers' only championship while in Brooklyn. Adding to the drama of Amoros' play was the fact that his catch could have only been made by a left-handed outfielder. The play reacquired Amoros to race toward the left field corner with his glove hand extended. It isn't likely that the right-handed Gilliam could have made the play.
8. False. Reggie Jackson and Mickey Mantle are tied for first with 18 postseason home runs.
9. False. Reggie Jackson was Kansas City's first-round pick and collected an $85,000 bonus.
10. True. Stan Musial had 1,377 extra base hits, 21 more than Babe Ruth.
11. True. Tom Seaver won 311 games.
12. True
13. False. The maximum bat length is 42 inches.
14. True. Dave Kingman hit 16 grand slam home runs, three more than Joe DiMaggio.
15. False. Babe Ruth and Henry Aaron each hit 13 grand slam home runs.
16. False. Ty Cobb was baseball's first MVP (1911).
17. True
18. True
19. True
20. True. Randy Johnson stands about 6'10".

HEAD-TO-HEAD IN THE NL OUTFIELD

Can you answer these 18 question about three standout National League outfielders and their 1993 seasons? The answers to questions 1-12 are found in the 1993 Box Score Comparison on the next page. Ten correct answers makes you a major-leaguer; 12 vaults you to all-star status.

a. Lenny Dykstra
    Philadelphia Phillies

b. Tony Gwynn
    San Diego Padres

c. Barry Bonds
    San Francisco Giants

1. Who had the highest batting average in 1993?

2. Who had the lowest batting average?

3. Who had the most at bats?

4. Who scored the most runs?

5. Who had the most hits?

6. Who had the most extra base hits (not including home runs)?

7. Who had the fewest extra base hits?

8. Who had the most home runs?

9. Who had the most RBI?

10. Who stole the most bases during the 1993 season?

11. Who had the fewest stolen bases?

EXTRA CREDIT
12. The combined errors of two of the outfielders equalled the total errors of the third. Who made the most errors?

13. Who won the batting title in 1987 with a .370 batting average?

14. Who won a National League batting title with a .313 average in 1988, the lowest winning average in National League history at the time?

15. Who was placed on probation for high stakes gambling in 1991 after he testified at the trial of a Mississippi man to losing $78,000 playing poker at an illegal casino?

16. Who led all 1986 rookies in home runs, RBI and steals?

17. Len Dykstra and a teammate were almost killed in a 1991 automobile accident. Dykstra was the driver; who was the passenger?

a. Milt Thompson
b. Terry Mulholland
c. Darren Daulton

18. Which all-star outfielder was not Rookie of the Year?

a. Len Dykstra
b. Tony Gwynn
c. Barry Bonds
d. none of the above

1993 Box Score Comparison

Player	AVG	AB	R	H	XBH	HR	RBI	S	E
a. Lenny Dykstra	.305	637	143	194	50	19	66	37	10
b. Tony Gwynn	.358	489	70	175	44	7	59	14	5
c. Barry Bonds	.336	529	129	181	44	46	123	29	5

Answers to questions 13-18:
13. b, Tony Gwynn; 14. b, Tony Gwynn; 15. a, Lenny Dykstra; 16. c, Barry Bonds; 17. c, Darren Daulton; 18. d, none of the above

Barry Bonds was the National League's Most Valuable Player in 1993.

THE FIRST WORLD SERIES

Can you answer these multiple choice questions about the first World Series? Eight correct answers makes you a major-leaguer; 11 vaults you to all-star status.

1. What teams met in the first World Series, played in 1903?

a. Boston/Pittsburgh
b. Philadelphia/Boston
c. Chicago/Cincinnati

2. What city hosted Game 1 of the first World Series?

a. Boston
b. Philadelphia
c. Chicago

3. How many games did the first World Series schedule call for?

a. Best of five
b. Best of seven
c. Best of nine

4. Who was the winning pitcher in Game 1?

a. Deacon Phillippe
b. Christy Mathewson
c. Nick Alrock

5. Who won the first World Series?

a. Boston
b. New York Giants
c. Chicago White Sox

6. At the time of the first World Series the American League was just three years old. How old was the National League?

a. 8
b. 18
c. 28

7. In 1903 Boston was not known as the Red Sox. What was its nickname?

a. Americans
b. Pilgrims
c. Yankees

8. Who threw the first pitch?

a. Norwood Gibson
b. Bill Dinneen
c. Cy Young

9. Boston used a five-man pitching staff that season, led by Cy Young and Bill Dinneen. During the eight-game series, two pitchers never played. A third pitched in only two innings and accumulated a 9.00 ERA. Who was he?

a. George Winter
b. "Long" Tom Hughes
c. Norwood Gibson

10. Who was the first pitcher to win three World Series games?

a. Cy Young
b. Deacon Phillippe
c. Bill Dinneen

11. Who equalled that record when he won Game 8?

a. Cy Young
b. Deacon Phillippe
c. Bill Dinneen

12. Who is the only pitcher to throw five complete games in the World Series?

a. Cy Young
b. Deacon Phillippe
c. Bill Dinneen

13. What was the approximate average attendance during the first World Series?

a. 21,000
b. 12,500
c. 2,100

14. Both the winners and the losers shared in the proceeds of that first World Series. The winners received approximately $1,200. Approximately how much did the losers receive?

a. $600
b. $1,200
c. $1,300

15. Who hit the first World Series home run?

a. Jimmy Sebring
b. Patsy Dougherty
c. Tommy Leach

1. a, Boston/Pittsburgh. The Pirates easily won the National League pennant in 1903, finishing seven games in front of the New York Giants. Pirates owner, Barney Dreyfuss, confident that he had the best team in baseball, challenged Boston owner Henry Killilea to a postseason best-of-nine World Series. They agreed to split the $55,500 in ticket sales. The New York Giants won the National League pennant in 1904 but Giants owner John Brush refused to play Boston, which had repeated in the American League.

2. a, Boston

3. c, best of nine

4. a, Deacon Phillippe put the Pirates ahead 1-0.

5. a, Boston won in eight games.

6. c, 28

7. b, Pilgrims. Give yourself credit if you answered "a" as well. The team was also referred to as the Americans at times because they played in the American League.

8. c, Cy Young. Young threw the first pitch but lost Game 1. On October 1, 1993, exactly 90 years after the first game of the 1903 World Series, the Boston Red Sox announced plans to erect a statue of Young on the same spot where he threw out the first pitch.

9. b, "Long" Tom Hughes. Both teams had excellent pitching. Boston featured 28-game winner Cy Young and 21-game winner Bill Dinneen. Pittsburgh's staff was equally impressive with 25-game winner Sam Leever, Deacon Phillippe (24) and Ed Doheny (16). Unfortunately for the Pirates, Leever was sidelined with a sore arm and Doheny had a nervous breakdown just prior to the start of the series. He went home to recuperate but became violent and attacked a male nurse with a poker, nearly killing him. Doheny was placed in an insane asylum

and never played baseball again. Without Leever and Doheny the Pirates were left with only one quality pitcher, Phillippe. He made a heroic effort, winning three games, including five complete games. His ERA was 2.86. Pittsburgh didn't sign more pitchers for the series because of an agreement between the owners prohibiting each club from acquiring a player after September 1; a World Series rule that still applies today.

10. b, Deacon Phillippe. Pittsburgh's Phillippe was the first pitcher to win three World Series games. He pitched a fourth time in Game 8, but lost 3-0 to Bill Dinneen.

11. c, Bill Dinneen
12. b, Deacon Phillippe
13. b, 12,500
14. c, $1,300. The losing Pirates received $1,316, $134 more than Boston's share. The reason: Pittsburgh owner Barney Dreyfuss gave his $6,700 share to his players; Boston owner Henry Killilea didn't.
15. a, Jimmy Sebring. The Pittsburgh No. 5 hitter hit the first World Series home run. It was against Cy Young in the first inning of Game 1.

WILD KINGDOM

Can you match the names of these pitchers with their animal kingdom nickname? Six correct answers makes you a major-leaguer; eight vaults you to all-star status.

NICKNAME

1. _____ Bulldog
2. _____ Mudcat
3. _____ The Bird
4. _____ The Vulture
5. _____ Moose
6. _____ Kitten
7. _____ The Big Bear
8. _____ Goose
9. _____ The Rat
10. _____ Catfish

GIVEN NAME

a. Jamie Easterly
b. Phil Regan
c. Mark Fidrych
d. Harvey Haddix
e. Bryan Haas
f. Mike Garcia
g. Orel Hershiser
h. Rich Gossage
i. Jim Grant
j. Jim Crawford

Answers: Wild Kingdom

1. g, Orel Hershiser. Hershiser's tenacity earned him the nickname "Bulldog" courtesy of Dodger Manager Tommy Lasorda. In 1988, Hershiser pitched 59 consecutive innings, surpassing Don Drysdale's streak by one inning on the last day of the season. He pitched another eight scoreless innings against the New York Mets during the play-offs, upping the streak to 67 innings.

2. i, Jim Grant. Grant was nicknamed "Mudcat" by Oakland owner Charlie Finley, who thought giving his pitchers nicknames was a good idea. Finley also thought orange baseballs, ball girls and a mechanical rabbit to deliver baseballs to umpires were good ideas, too. Finley's Athletics won five straight division titles and three World Championships between 1971 and 1975.

3. b, Phil Regan

4. c, Mark Fidrych. Fidrych went 19-9 with a 2.34 ERA and was named Rookie of the Year in 1976 as a member of the Detroit Tigers. Unfortunately it was "The Bird's" only good year. A year later he developed arm trouble and won only 10 more games during his career.

5. e, Bryan Haas

6. d, Harvey Haddix was nicknamed "Kitten" because of his resemblance to another pitcher, Harry "The Cat" Brecheen.

7. f, Mike Garcia

8. h, Rich Gossage

9. a, Jamie Easterly

10. j, Jim Crawford

KNUCKLING DOWN

Can you answer these multiple choice and true/false questions about knuckleball pitchers? Ten correct answers makes you a major-leaguer; 12 vaults you to all-star status.

1. Who was the first knuckleball pitcher to be inducted into the Baseball Hall of Fame?

a. Emil "Dutch" Leonard
b. Wilbur Wood
c. Hoyt Wilhelm

2. Who won more than 300 games during his career?

a. Emil "Dutch" Leonard
b. Phil Niekro
c. Wilbur Wood

3. Who twice led the league with 24 wins?

a. Wilbur Wood
b. Roger Wolff
c. Emil "Dutch" Leonard

4. Who twice led the league with the lowest ERA?

a. Phil Niekro
b. Johnny Niggeling
c. Hoyt Wilhelm

5. Who set the record for most appearances by a pitcher with 1,070?

a. Wilbur Wood
b. Hoyt Wilhelm
c. Phil Niekro

6. Who was nicknamed "Knucksie"?

a. Joe Kiekro
b. Phil Niekro
c. Charlie Hough

7. True or false: Wilbur Wood pitched in two World Series with two different teams during his 18-year career?

8. True or false: Charlie Hough was originally signed by the Dodgers as a third baseman.

9. True or false: Hoyt Wilhelm and Tommy Lasorda taught Charlie Hough how to throw the knuckleball.

10. Which of the following pitchers was used almost exclusively as a reliever throughout his career, compared to the other two who were utilized mostly as starters?

a. Joe Niekro
b. Wilbur Wood
c. Hoyt Wilhelm

11. Which of these knuckleballers won the fewest games?

a. Hoyt Wilhelm
b. Wilbur Wood
c. Emil "Dutch" Leonard

12. Who regularly pitched with only two days rest when used as a starter?

a. Joe Niekro
b. Wilbur Wood
c. Charlie Hough

13. True or false: Joe Niekro and his brother, Phil, pitched for the New York Yankees.

14. True or false: Neither Joe Niekro nor his brother, Phil, ever pitched in a World Series.

15. True or false: Upon his retirement in 1972, Hoyt Wilhelm established the major league record for most games pitched in relief (1,018).

16. True or false: Hoyt Wilhelm set records for games completed by a pitcher (651) and total innings pitched by a reliever (1,870).

Answers: Knuckling Down

1. c, Emil "Dutch" Leonard
2. b, Phil Niekro won 318 games. The others won less than 300.
3. a, Wilbur Wood won 24 games in 1972 and 1973 with the Chicago White Sox.
4. c, Hoyt Wilhelm had the league's lowest ERA in 1952 and 1959. Johnny Niggeling did not make it to the major leagues until he was 35 years old. He came up with the Boston Braves in 1938 and later pitched with the Reds, Browns and Washington Senators before retiring at age 43. Lifetime he was 64-69 with a 3.22 ERA.
5. b, Hoyt Wilhelm
6. b, Phil Niekro
7. False. Wilbur Wood played for the Red Sox, Pirates and White Sox, but never played in a World Series.
8. True
9. True
10. c, Hoyt Wilhelm
11. a, Hoyt Wilhelm won 143 games, Wilbur Wood 164 and Emil "Dutch" Leonard 191.

At the end of his second season with the Dodgers in 1936, Leonard was stricken with arm problems. He spent the next two years in the minors where he learned to throw the knuckler. He returned to the majors with the Washington Senators where he quickly established himself as an effective pitcher thanks to the knuckleball. In 1945 the Senators' pitching staff included Leonard, Roger Wolff, Mickey Haefner and Johnny Niggeling - all knuckleball pitchers. Lifetime, Leonard was 191-181 with a 3.25 ERA. Toward the end of his career Leonard became a reliever with the Cubs. On one memorable occasion he came into a game against the Dodgers in the bottom of the ninth inning with nobody out, the bases loaded and the Cubs ahead by a run. Leonard retired Jackie Robinson, Gil Hodges and Roy Campanella in order.

There was another "Dutch" Leonard who pitched before Emil. The elder Leonard pitched in the American League from 1913-25. Hubert "Dutch" Leonard won 129 games during his career, including three no-hitters. In 1914, Leonard had a major league record 1.01 ERA. In 1924, while pitching with the Tigers under Manager Ty Cobb, Leonard developed arm problems which forced him to leave the game within two years.

Leonard blamed Cobb for his fall from baseball, saying Cobb played him too often. Leonard retaliated against Cobb in 1927 by releasing two letters that implicated Cobb, "Smokey" Joe Wood and Tris Speaker – all future Hall of Famers – in a scheme to fix a game played in 1919. Leonard claimed he and Cobb conspired with Cleveland's Speaker and Wood to fix a game in favor of the Tigers so they would clinch third place behind Chicago and Cleveland, thus making Detroit eligible for a share of the World Series purse. The Tigers won the game 9-5. After trying unsuccessfully to sell the incriminating letters to the media, Leonard turned them over to American League President Ban Johnson. Johnson tried to cover up the scandal by teaming with Detroit owner Frank Navin to pay Leonard more than $10,000 for the letters and his silence. Johnson met with Cobb and Speaker, who agreed to resign from their positions as managers in exchange for Johnson keeping the episode quiet. Johnson later reneged on the deal and informed the baseball club presidents of the situation. The presidents decided to turn the evidence over to Commissioner Judge Kennesaw Mountain Landis. Landis, brought charges against Cobb and Speaker (Wood was already out of baseball). Wood, Speaker and Cobb appeared at a hearing before Landis where they denied the charges. Leonard refused to travel from his home in California to appear at the hearing in Chicago.

Landis mulled over his decision for two months before ruling the evidence wasn't solid enough to implicate Cobb and Speaker. Cobb and Speaker returned to baseball as players for a short time, but were never asked to manage again.

12. b, Wilbur Wood
13. True. Charlie Hough was used as a reliever when he pitched for the Dodgers between 1970 and 1978. In 1976 he led the National League with 12 relief wins. It was not until he was traded to Texas that he became a starter. Hough led the Rangers in innings pitched, complete games and wins between 1982 and 1987. In 1987 Hough became the oldest pitcher in American League history to lead the league in starts and innings pitched. In 1993 he led the expansion Florida Marlins in innings pitched (204), wins (nine) and strikeouts (126).
14. False. Joe Niekro appeared in the 1987 World Series with the Minnesota Twins, who lost in seven games to the St. Louis Cardinals.
15. True
16. True

MINDING YOUR P's & Q's

Can you match the players with their descriptions? All the last names begin with P or Q. Seven correct answers makes you a major-leaguer; 10 vaults you to all-star status.

a. Kirby Puckett   e. Lou Piniella   i. Dan Quisenberry

b. Rico Petrocelli   f. Bruce Petway   j. Luis Polonia

c. Johnny Pesky   g. Jimmy Piersall   k. Jamie Quirk

d. Mel Queen   h. Joe Pepitone   l. Tony Phillips

1. This father and son pitching combination shared the same first and last name but different fates on the hill. Dad emerged with the Yankees in 1942 and later played with the Pirates. Lifetime he was 27-40 with a 5.09 ERA. Son fared somewhat better as a starter for the Reds and later as a reliever with the Angels between 1966 and 1972. Lifetime he was 20-17 with a 3.14 ERA.

_____

2. This player nicknamed "Quiz" was a premier reliever in the American League during the 1980s. He led the league in saves and was named the "Fireman of the Year" by *The Sporting News* five times. Well ahead of the big-money contracts of the 1990s, Kansas City signed this ace reliever to a $30 million guaranteed lifetime contract.

_____

3. This minor league shortstop came up with the Royals in 1975, primarily playing third base. Five seasons later he switched to catcher. Lifetime he hit just .237, but his real value was in his defensive skills and ability to throw out would-be base stealers. He finished his career in 1989 with the Yankees as a backup catcher.

_____

4. In 1963 this rookie first baseman replaced Bill "Moose" Skowron in the New York Yankee infield. In his first season he hit over .270 with 27 HRs and 89 RBI. He won three Gold Gloves and hit more than 200 HRs during his career. The Yankees traded him in 1969 to the Astros for Curt Blefary. He finished his career in Japan.

_____

5. This accident-prone infielder came up in 1983 as a second baseman with Oakland. In 1985 he broke his foot twice and in 1987 broke his wrist thanks to a Mark McGuire line drive during batting practice. He was the first Oakland player to hit for the cycle and set a World Series record in 1989 when he played second base, third base and in left field during Game 3.

_____

6. This infielder broke into the majors with the Red Sox in 1965 and soon shared the American League record for fewest errors by a shortstop (14). In 1971 he moved to third base after Luis Aparicio joined the team. He immediately led the American League in fielding percentage at his new position. During his 12-year career he hit 210 home runs.

_____

7. Born Michael Paveskovich, this infielder led the American League in hits with 207 and had a .331 batting average in his first season (1942), second only to teammate Ted Williams' .356. Playing both shortstop and third base, he stabilized the Red Sox infield until being traded during the 1952 season. He eventually returned to Boston as a manager and broadcaster. He is still with the organization.

_____

8. This outfielder doesn't have a reputation as an outstanding fielder, but always seems to get the job done. Considered an excellent contact hitter, he routinely hits around .300 and has a career batting average around .335 with two outs and runners in scoring position. He came up with Oakland and was traded to the Yankees in 1989 as part of the Rickey Henderson exchange. The Yankees later traded him to the Angels.

_____

9. This outstanding fielder replaced Dom DiMaggio in the Red Sox outfield in 1962 and played the shallowest center field in the majors. During his career he won two Gold Gloves, was an all-star twice and had a career .272 batting average. Toward the end of his career he played for Cleveland, Washington, New York Mets and California Angels. His reputation as an excellent fielding outfielder is unfortunately over-shadowed by his reputation as an eccentric.

_____

10. This Minnesota Twins outfielder was Rookie of the Year in 1984. In 1992 he became a free agent, but his loyalty to the Twins and the City of Minnesota meant more to him than the lucrative offer Boston made to acquire his services.

_____

11. This outfielder was originally drafted as a Washington Senator in the early 1960s, but made his reputation as a clutch hitter with the Yankees, playing the outfield and as a designated hitter. Owner George Steinbrenner kept him on with the organization after retirement as a coach and later as manager. Eventually he moved on to manage teams in both leagues.

_____

12. This catcher was never given the opportunity to play in the majors because he was black. He proved worthy of a shot at the majors during a series against the Detroit Tigers in 1910. The games were played in Cuba, and he hit .412 while throwing out numerous would-be base stealers, including Ty Cobb. He's believed to be the first catcher to throw to second from the squatting position. He played professionally and later as a player-manager until retiring in 1925.

_____

Answers: Minding Your P's & Q's

1. d, Mel Queen
2. i, Dan Quisenberry
3. k, Jamie Quirk
4. h, Joe Pepitone
5. l, Tony Phillips
6. b, Rico Petrocelli
7. c, Johnny Pesky
8. j, Luis Polonia
9. g, Jimmy Piersall
10. a, Kirby Puckett
11. e, Lou Piniella

12. f, Bruce Petway. In 1910 many of the best black ballplayers played in the integrated Cuban Winter League. A classic matchup took place in November of 1910 between Hall of Famer Ty Cobb and Bruce Petway. Petway threw Cobb out attempting to steal three times in a row. Legend says on Cobb's third attempt he didn't even bother to run all the way to second after seeing the ball waiting for him at the bag. He merely turned and trotted off the field instead.

MINDING YOUR P's & Q's
(PART II)

Can you answer these true/false questions about players whose last names begin with P or Q? Eight correct answers makes you a major-leaguer; 11 vaults you to all-star status.

1. Melido Perez was signed by the Chicago White Sox in 1983.

2. Melido Perez was traded to the New York Yankees in exchange for second baseman Steve Sax.

3. Boog Powell, played for the Orioles, Indians and Dodgers.

4. Boog Powell is the Oriole's all-time home run leader.

5. Joe Quinn, who played and managed from 1884 to 1901, was the first native Australian to play in the major leagues.

6. Luis Quinones backed up third baseman Chris Sabo during Cincinnati's 1989 season. He had 24 hits and 12 HRs in 340 at bats.

7. Jamie Quirk's real name is Fred.

8. Terry Puhl hit .568 in the 1980 National League Championship Series, a record for a five-game series.

9. Right-handed Met pitcher Charlie Puleo was once traded for Tom Seaver.

10. Dick Pole, who pitched for the Red Sox and the Mariners from 1973-78, was Seattle's pitching coach in 1993.

11. Umpire Jim Quick once ejected a trainer from a game.

12. Gaylord Perry won his 300th game while pitching for Atlanta.

13. Rico Petrocelli set an American League single season record for the most home runs by a shortstop when he hit 40 in 1969.

14. Pitchers Stan Perzanowski and Ron Perranoski are cousins.

Answers: Minding Your P's & Q's (Part II)

1. False. Melido Perez was originally signed by Kansas City in 1983. Four years later he was the winning pitcher against the Chicago White Sox in his major league debut. Later that year he was traded to the Sox.
2. True
3. True. Boog Powell was a standout player for the Orioles from 1961 to 1974. He was traded to the Indians for Dave Duncan where he played for two years. He spent his last year as a pinch-hitter with the Dodgers.
4. False. Boog Powell trails Eddie Murray.
5. True
6. True
7. False
8. True
9. True. In 1982 the Mets traded Charlie Puleo and two minor leaguers to the Reds and reacquired Tom Seaver. In 1983 Seaver was 9-14 with a 3.55 ERA.
10. False. Dick Pole was the pitching coach for the San Francisco Giants in 1993.
11. True. In a rain-soaked game between Cincinnati and Atlanta in 1985, the Reds trainer was tossed out of the game for shouting to Umpire Jim Quick, "Why don't you stop the game before someone gets hurt?"
12. False. Gaylord Perry won his 300th game while pitching for Seattle in 1982.
13. True
14. True. Stan Perzanowski was 5-11 with a 5.11 ERA during his career, while his cousin Ron Perranoski was 79-74 with a 2.79 ERA and 179 saves.

THE 200/40 CLUB

Can you answer these multiple choice questions about players who totaled 200 hits and 40 home runs in the same season? Four correct answers makes you a major-leaguer; five vaults you to all-star status.

1. Who was the first player in major league history to have at least 200 hits and 40 home runs in the same season?

a. Rogers Hornsby
b. Babe Ruth
c. Chuck Klein

2. Who had five seasons with at least 200 hits and 40 home runs?

a. Jimmie Foxx
b. Babe Ruth
c. Lou Gehrig

3. Who was the last player to collect 200 hits and 40 homers in a single season?

a. Reggie Jackson
b. Jim Rice
c. George Foster

4. Who was the last Yankee to have 200 hits with 40 home runs?

a. Joe DiMaggio
b. Mickey Mantle
c. Roger Maris

5. Which one of the following American Leaguers never had a season with at least 200 hits that included 40 or more home runs?

a. Hank Greenberg
b. Hal Trosky
c. Al Rosen
d. Frank Robinson

6. Who was the last National Leaguer to have 200 hits with 40 homers?

a. Bobby Bonds
b. Frank Robinson
c. Billy Williams
d. Mike Schmidt

7. Which one of the following National Leaguers never had a season with 200 or more hits that included at least 40 home runs?

a. Hank Aaron
b. Duke Snider
c. Chuck Klein

Answers: The 200/40 Club

1. b, Babe Ruth had 204 hits and 50 HRs in 1921.
2. c, Lou Gehrig had at least 200 hits and 40 HRs in 1927, 1930-31, 1934 and 1936; Babe Ruth in 1921, 1923 and 1924; and Jimmie Foxx in 1932 and 1933.
3. b, Red Sox outfielder Jim Rice had 213 hits and 46 HRs in 1978.
4. a, in 1937, Joe DiMaggio hit 46 HRs among his 215 hits.
5. d, Frank Robinson never had a season that included 200 or more hits with 40 homers. Hank Greenberg just made it in 1937, hitting both numbers right on the nose.
6. c, Billy Williams had 205 hits with 42 HRs in 1970.
7. b, Dodger Duke Snider never had 200 hits with 40 home runs in a single season, although he usually finished at or near the top of the National League in batting average, hits, RBI and home runs. During the 1950s, Snyder hit more homers than anyone (326). The most he had in one season was 56. Hank Aaron had 201 hits and 44 HRs with the Milwaukee Braves in 1963. Chuck Klein did it in 1929 (219, 43) and 1930 (250, 40).

SAYONARA USA

Can you answer these multiple choice questions about players who left the United States to play in Japan? Three correct answers makes you a major-leaguer; four vaults you to all-star status.

1. In Japan, what do fans call American baseball players?

a. Hung Shu
b. Gaijin
c. Hoisin

2. Former Cleveland and New York Yankee outfielder Mel Hall signed with a Japanese team for the 1993 and '94 seasons. How much will he be paid over those two years?

a. $400,000
b. $1,400,000
c. $4,000,000

3. Twenty-five former major leaguers played in Japan in 1993. How many were either pitchers or catchers?

a. 0
b. 1
c. 10

4. Of the 25 former major leaguers playing in Japan in 1993, how many were infielders?

a. 4
b. 8
c. 12

5. Of the 25 former major leaguers playing in Japan in 1993, how many were outfielders?

a. 5
b. 10
c. 15

Answers: Sayonara USA

1. b, Gaijin.
2. c, $4,000,000
3. b, 1
4. b, 8
5. c, 15

Clearly, Cecil Fielder has established himself as the best Japanese-American transplant in baseball. Fielder originally came up through the Toronto organization in 1985 and hit .311 his first year. His productivity diminished over the next three seasons, however, and the Blue Jays sold his contract to the Hanshin Tigers in Japan after the 1988 season. Fielder returned to the United States in 1990, this time with the Detroit Tigers, and led the league in home runs and RBI in 1990 and '91.

TOEING THE SLAB

Can you answer these multiple choice questions about pitching? Twelve correct answers makes you a major-leaguer; 15 vaults you to all-star status.

1. What is the winningest brother pitching combination in major league baseball history?

a. Phil and Joe Niekro
b. Dizzy and Paul Dean
c. Gaylord and Jim Perry

2. Who was the first relief pitcher inducted into the Baseball Hall of Fame?

a. Rollie Fingers
b. Joe Page
c. Hoyt Wilhelm
d. Ace Adams

3. Who set the major league record for wins by a relief pitcher (123)?

a. Jim Konstanty
b. Hoyt Wilhelm
c. Elroy Face

4. In 1987, who became the oldest pitcher in American League history to lead the league in starts and innings pitched?

a. Charlie Hough
b. Phil Niekro
c. Nolan Ryan

5. Nolan Ryan was the all-time strikeout leader long before his retirement. How many batters did Nolan Ryan strike out during his career?

a. 4,136
b. 5,001
c. 5,714

6. Nolan Ryan had more strikeouts than any other pitcher when he retired in 1993. Who is No. 2 on the strikeout list?

a. Cy Young
b. Walter Johnson
c. Steve Carlton

7. Who did Yankee pitcher Dave Righetti no-hit on July 4th, 1983?

a. White Sox
b. Red Sox
c. Brewers

8. Who is the only Yankee to ever throw two no-hitters during his career in New York?

a. Allie Reynolds
b. Don Larsen
c. Mel Stottlemyre

9. Who was the first pitcher to be inducted into the Baseball Hall of Fame with fewer than 150 wins?

a. Hoyt Wilhelm
b. Sandy Koufax
c. Rollie Fingers

10. What Cleveland Indian pitcher totalled a rookie record 245 strikeouts?

a. Bob Feller
b. Gary Bell
c. Herb Score

11. Who was the only relief pitcher to be traded during a season in which he already had at least 30 saves?

a. Bruce Sutter
b. Jeff Reardon
c. Lee Smith

12. Who were the first brothers to pitch against each other as major league rookies?

a. Todd and Mel Stottlemyre, Jr.
b. Joe and Phil Niekro
c. Greg and Mike Maddux

13. Who is the only pitcher to win Rookie of the Year, MVP the Cy Young honors?

a. Don Newcome
b. Roger Clemens
c. Bob Gibson

14. The American League record of eight consecutive strikeouts is shared by three pitchers (two starters and a reliever). Who is the reliever?

a. Goose Gossage
b. Ron Davis
c. Dick Radatz

15. What former pitcher and current pitching coach lost 20 games a year after winning 20?

a. Galen Cisco
b. Mel Stottlemyre
c. Dick Pole

16. Who holds the record for picking off three baserunners in the same inning?

a. Warren Spahn
b. Tippy Martinez
c. Steve Carlton

17. Two starting pitchers share the American League record with a reliever for striking out eight consecutive batters. Which of the following is not one of the starters?

a. Randy Johnson
b. Roger Clemens
c. Nolan Ryan

18. Who, in 1980, became the first pitcher to earn $1 million for a single season?

a. Doyle Alexander
b. Tom Seaver
c. Nolan Ryan

19. Nolan Ryan is second only to Cy Young in career starts by a pitcher (818). Who is third on the list?

a. Walter Johnson
b. Don Sutton
c. Gaylord Perry

Answers: Toeing the Slab

1. a, Phil and Joe Niekro combined for 538 wins. Gaylord and Jim Perry are second with 529. Dizzy and Paul Dean totalled 200 (150 by Dizzy).
2. c, Hoyt Wilhelm was inducted into the Hall of Fame in 1985. Rollie Fingers followed five years later.
3. b, Hoyt Wilhelm
4. a, Charlie Hough. Hough was 39 when he led the American League in starts and innings pitched. Hough, a member of the Texas Rangers, contributed to another record that season. Texas catchers set a major league record for the most passed balls in a season with 73. Hough contributed 65.
5. c, 5,714
6. c, Nolan Ryan had 5,714 strikeouts during his career; Steve Carlton, 4,136.
7. b, Red Sox
8. a, Allie Reynolds
9. a, Hoyt Wilhelm
10. c, A line drive back to the mound ended Herb Score's promising career. He won 16 games and struck out 245 batters as a rookie in 1955. In 1956 he won 20 games, including five shutouts and 263 strikeouts. On May 27, 1957, Score was struck in the eye by a line drive off the bat of New York Yankee Gil McDougald. There was concern that Score would never regain his sight in the eye. He eventually returned to the Indians but struggled in Cleveland and later with the Chicago White Sox. He retired in 1962, having won just 19 games his last seven seasons. Today, Score is the play-by-play announcer for Indians radio broadcasts.
11. c, Lee Smith
12. c, Greg and Mike Maddox
13. a, Don Newcome
14. b, Ron Davis
15. b, Mel Stottlemyre was 20-9 with the Yankees in 1965, and led the American league with 20 losses in 1966 (12-20).
16. b, Tippy Martinez
17. a, Randy Johnson. The record is shared by Ron Davis, Nolan Ryan and Roger Clemens.
18. c, Nolan Ryan was a member of the Houston Astros in 1980 when he became the first pitcher to earn $1 million for one season. In May of 1982, Yankee pitcher Doyle Alexander was taken out of the game by Manager Gene Michael. Alexander didn't agree with the decision and punched a wall in the dugout, breaking his hand. Afterward Michael said "It was a dumb thing to do, one of the dumbest things I've ever seen." Alexander offered to go without pay during the five weeks he was unable to pitch. The players' union, however, challenged the decision, fearing a precedent was being set that would adversely affect other injured players in the future. The case went to arbitration and the players' union won, forcing Alexander to accept a paycheck while his broken hand healed.
19. c, Gaylord Perry

HEAD-TO-HEAD AT FIRST BASE

Can you answer these 18 questions about three standout first basemen and their 1993 seasons? The answers to questions 1-14 are found in the 1993 Box Score Comparison on the next page. Eight correct answers makes you a major-leaguer; 10 vaults you to all-star status.

a. Don Mattingly
   New York Yankees

b. Fred McGriff
   Atlanta Braves

c. Frank Thomas
   Chicago White Sox

1. Who hit over .300?

2. Who had the fewest at bats?

3. Who scored the fewest runs?

4. Who scored the most runs?

5. The trio totalled extra base hits within six of each other (not including home runs). Within what range did they fall?

a. 0-25
b. 25-37
c. 38 or more

6. Who had the most hits?

7. Who had the fewest hits?

8. Who hit the most home runs?

9. Who hit the fewest home runs?

10. Who drove in the most runs?

11. Who had the fewest RBI?

12. Who failed to steal a base?

13. Who made the fewest errors?

14. Who made the most errors?

EXTRA CREDIT
15. Who was not originally signed by the New York Yankees?

16. Who led the American League in home runs in 1989 with 36?

17. Who tied a major league record with 22 putouts in a nine-inning game?

18. Who was a designated hitter as a rookie?

Player	AVG	AB	R	H	XBH	HR	RBI	S	E
a. Don Mattingly	.291	530	78	154	29	17	86	0	3
b. Fred McGriff	.291	557	111	162	31	37	101	5	17
c. Frank Thomas	.316	545	106	172	35	41	126	4	15

Answers to questions 15-18:
15. c, Frank Thomas; 16. b, Fred McGriff; 17. a, Don Mattingly; 18. b, Fred McGriff

YOU MAKE THE CALL

Can you answer these multiple choice questions that pertain to the rules of baseball? Sixteen correct answers makes you a major-leaguer; 19 vaults you to all-star status.

1. As the pitcher goes into his windup the third base umpire calls time-out. The pitcher, unable to stop his momentum, continues his motion to the plate. The batter hits a fly ball that is caught. What happens?

a. no pitch
b. the batter is out
c. neither a nor b

2. The distance from the pitching rubber to home plate is 60 feet, 6 inches, but that hasn't always been the official measurement. What was it before being altered to its present distance?

a. 48 feet, 6 inches
b. 50 feet
c. 55 feet, 6 inches

3. The count is two balls and one strike on the batter with a runner on first base. The pitcher accidently drops the ball while standing on the rubber. What happens?

a. nothing
b. it's a pitch and called a ball
c. it's a balk and the runner advances to second base

4. There is a full count on the batter with no one on base. The pitcher accidently drops the ball while standing on the rubber. What happens?

a. nothing
b. it's a pitch and called a ball
c. neither a nor b

5. The count is one ball and one strike to the batter with a runner on first base. Mistaking the third base coach for a baserunner, the pitcher steps off the rubber and throws to the third baseman. What happens?

a. nothing
b. a balk is called and the runner advances to second base
c. it's a pitch and called a ball
d. none of the above

6. In addition to the home plate umpire, how many umpires work a normal major-league game?

a. 2
b. 3
c. 4

7. The pitcher throws the ball on a 25 foot arc to the batter. It comes down belt high, directly over the plate. What's the call?

a. no pitch
b. illegal pitch
c. strike

8. The pitcher brushes back the batter with a fastball high and inside. The next pitch is a slow curve, again inside. The batter disdainfully reaches out, catches the slow curve and throws it back to the pitcher. What happens?

a. no pitch
b. ball
c. strike

9. What year was it ruled illegal to throw a pitch solely for the purpose of knocking down a batter?

a. 1881
b. 1901
c. 1921

10. Following a home run, the pitcher's next pitch is dangerously high and inside to the batter. The umpire is convinced the pitch was intentionally thrown to harm the batter. What happens?

a. the pitcher receives a warning
b. the pitcher and his manager receive a warning
c. the pitcher and both managers receive a warning

11. In a continuation of Question 11: The roles are now reversed, with the team that hit the home run now in the field. The pitcher appears to retaliate with a brushback pitch to the lead off batter. This too seems intentional to the umpire. What happens?

a. the pitcher is warned
b. the pitcher and his manager are warned
c. the pitcher is ejected from the game

12. How many throws is a pitcher allowed when warming up before each inning?

a. 5
b. 8
c. 10

13. How many throws is a relief pitcher allowed when he enters a game?

a. 5
b. 8
c. 10

14. The rule book states the home plate umpire may dictate how much time a pitcher is allowed between pitches. What is the maximum amount of time allowed?

a. 20 seconds
b. 30 seconds
c. 45 seconds

15. What year was the spitball banned?

a. 1920
b. 1935
c. 1947

16. What happens if a pitcher inadvertently licks his fingers with runners on base?

a. it's a ball
b. it's a balk and the runners advance one base
c. it's a balk, the runners advance one base and a ball is added to the batter's count
d. nothing

17. In a continuation of question 18: What if the bases are empty?

a. nothing
b. it's a ball
c. it's an automatic walk

18. In 1903, the official height of the pitching mound was established at 15 inches above the baselines. The rule was revised in 1969 to what present-day height?

a. 10 inches
b. 12 inches
c. 16 inches

19. The umpire suspects the pitcher of throwing illegal pitches and inspects the ball for scuff marks. He doesn't find any but issues a warning to the pitcher. The umpire is still suspicious and is later convinced the pitcher is throwing spitballs. What can the umpire do?

a. nothing
b. warn the pitcher again
c. eject the pitcher from the game

Anwers: You Make the Call

1. a, no pitch. When the umpire calls time-out, play stops immediately whether anyone heard him or not. Therefore, when the umpire calls time-out but the pitcher is unable to stop his momentum, the pitch doesn't count.

2. b, 50 feet. The original distance was 35 feet and pitches were delivered underhanded. The distance was later changed to 45 feet and then to 50 feet. The current distance was supposed to be just 60 feet, but some-one misread the dimensions and placed the pitching rubber six additional inches fur-ther from home plate. No one objected to the mistake, so the distance was kept at 60 feet, 6 inches.

3. c, it's a balk and the runner advances to sec-ond base.

4. b, it's a pitch and called a ball.

5. b, a balk is called and the runner advances to second base.

6. b, 3. In 1952, four umpires became the stan-dard for a regular season game. When New York Yankee Don Larsen pitched his per-fect game in the 1956 World Series against the Brooklyn Dodgers, umpire Babe Pinelli was behind the plate. He retired two days later. Pinelli had umpired in the National League for 22 years.

7. c, strike. There is nothing in the rule book regarding the trajectory of pitches. Rip Sewell is credited with inventing the arc pitch in 1943. Dick Wakefield was the bat-ter when Sewell first used the pitch and struck out. The pitch soon became known as "The Ephus" but no one knows why. It took three years for anyone to hit a home run off a "Ephus" pitch. During the 1946 All-Star Game, Sewell threw his trick pitch to Ted Williams, who hit it into the right field bleachers.

8. c, strike.

9. a, 1881. Cleveland Indian shortstop Ray Chapman is the only person every killed by a pitch in a major league game. Yankee pitcher Carl Mays made the fatal toss on August 16, 1920. Chapman's death didn't seem to bother Mays the remainder of the season. He finished with a 26-11 record, and was 27-9 with a .343 batting average the next year.

10. c, the pitcher and both managers receive a warning.

11. c, the pitcher is ejected from the game. Be-cause his manager was already warned, the pitcher is ejected. Casey Stengel suggested the rule be changed from awarding first base to the batter to letting him advance all the way to third. This would immediately put the beaned batter in scoring position and also allow anyone on base at the time of the pitch to score.

12. b, 8. A pitcher is entitled one minute or eight warmup throws. If a pitcher suddenly leaves a game due to injury there is no limit to the number of pitches his replacement may throw.

13. b, 8. Same explanation as Question 12.

14. a, 20 seconds. The rule is frequently vio-lated and rarely enforced by umpires.

15. a, the rule went into effect in 1920, but be-cause there were so many spitball pitchers around the league they had to be phased out. Therefore, teams were allowed to re-tain two spitball pitchers for the 1920 sea-son. In 1921, 17 pitchers (nine in the Ameri-can League) were officially designated as "spitball pitchers" and allowed to use the "spitter" for the rest of their careers.

16. b, it's a balk and the runners advance one base.

17. b, it's a ball.

18. a, 10 inches.

19. c, umpires can eject pitchers from the game without evidence, but only after issuing a warning.

1993 WORLD SERIES

Can you answer these multiple choice and true/false questions about the 1993 World Series? Eleven correct answers makes you a major-leaguer; 14 vaults you to all-star status.

1. Who was the MVP?

a. Joe Carter
b. Paul Molitor
c. Roberto Alomar

2. Who totalled a series-high nine RBI for Toronto?

a. Tony Fernandez
b. Paul Molitor
c. Joe Carter

3. What pitcher established a World Series record by walking four batters in the same inning?

a. Mitch Williams
b. Todd Stottlemyre
c. Tommy Greene

4. Who was the only player (with at least 15 at bats) to hit less than .100?

a. Ed Sprague
b. Darren Daulton
c. Pat Borders

5. Who scored the most runs for Philadelphia?

a. Jim Eisenreich
b. John Kruk
c. Lenny Dykstra

6. What Philadelphia reliever had the highest ERA during the Series?

a. Larry Anderson
b. Mitch Williams
c. David West

7. True or false: Toronto's John Olerud hit under .250 during the Series.

8. True or false: Blue Jay pitcher Al Leiter batted 1.000 during the Series.

9. True or false: Every Philadelphia starter (except pitchers) had at least one RBI during the Series.

10. True or false: Every Toronto starter (except pitchers) had at least one RBI during the Series.

11. Who was the only Toronto pitcher to have an ERA in double figures?

a. Al Leiter
b. Todd Stottlemyre
c. Duane Ward

12. Who was the only pitcher to throw a complete game shutout?

a. Terry Mulholland
b. Curt Schilling
c. Tommy Greene

13. Toronto committed seven errors during the Series; three players committed two apiece. Who committed only one?

a. Joe Carter
b. Robbie Alomar
c. Ed Sprague
d. Pat Borders

14. True or false: No pitcher drove in any runs.

15. True or false: Toronto had a better fielding percentage than Philadelphia.

16. True or false: Toronto's ERA was 5.77.

17. True or false: Every Philadelphia pitcher walked at least one batter.

18. True or false: Philadelphia pitchers walked more batters than Toronto pitchers.

19. True or false: Both teams hit over .300.

20. Which pitching staff recorded the most strikeouts?

a. Philadelphia
b. Toronto
c. They were even

Answers: 1993 World Series

1. b, Paul Molitor was signed by the Blue Jays as a replacement for former designated hitter Dave Winfield. Winfield left Toronto at the end of the 1992 season because the front office refused to offer the aging veteran a three-year contract. Molitor came to Toronto from Milwaukee. The Brewers lost Moliter when owner Bud Selig offered him $1.2 million less than the previous year – this after Moliter hit .320 in 1992. Molitor hadn't planned to leave Milwaukee, but was so insulted by Selig's offer that he decided to test the market. The Blue Jays quickly signed Molitor before Selig came to his senses. Gillik was rewarded handsomely as Molitor had one of his best seasons. The 37-year-

old hit .322 during the season, including 22 HRs. He batted .384 with runners in scoring position; .391 during the American League Championship Series; and .500 (12 for 24) in the World Series.
2. a, Tony Fernandez
3. b, Todd Stottlemyer
4. a, Ed Sprague had one hit in 15 at bats (.067).
5. c, Lenny Dykstra
6. c, David West had an ERA of 27.00.
7. True, John Olerud, who hit more than 100 points higher during the season, was 4 for 17 (.235).
8. True, Al Leiter was 1 for 1 (1.000).
9. True
10. True

11. b, Todd Stottlemyre's ERA was 27.00 during the World Series.
12. b, Curt Schilling
13. c, Ed Sprague
14. True
15. Philadelphia had a .991 fielding percentage, 24 points higher than Toronto.

16. True
17. True
18. False, Toronto pitchers recorded 34 walks; Philadelphia 25.
19. False, Toronto hit .311; Philadelphia .274.
20. a, Philadelphia batters struck out 50 times, Toronto 30.

THE AMERICAN LEAGUE

Can you answer these true/false questions about the American League? Eight correct answers makes you a major-leaguer; 11 vaults you to all-star status.

1. An American League attendance record was set during the last weekend of the 1993 season when a total of 216,904 fans paid to watch a three-game series between the White Sox and Indians in Cleveland.

2. In Kansas City's last game of the 1993 season, George Brett hit a game-winning home run during his last career at bat.

3. In 1972, Oakland owner Charlie Finley gave a $3,000 bonus to his players if they grew mustaches.

4. Carlos May, an all-star in 1969 as a rookie with the White Sox, wore his birth date on the back of his uniform.

5. In 1958, former Baltimore Oriole General Manager Paul Richards developed an oversized catcher's mitt to use when knuckleball pitcher Hoyt Wilhelm was on the mound.

6. Former Giant General Manager and Cleveland Indian third baseman Al Rosen set an American League record when he hit 37 HRs as a rookie. Rosen was an all-star twice and led the league in RBI twice, but was never named MVP.

7. New York Yankee Billy Martin's 40-year-old American League record of 10 hits in the World Series fell during the 1993 Toronto/Philadelphia series.

8. Billy Martin was the first player to get two hits in one inning as a rookie playing in his first game.

9. Yogi Berra won the American League pennant in his first year as the Yankees' manager in 1964, but lost the World Series in seven games to the St. Louis Cardinals.

10. Billy Martin once wrote that Joe DiMaggio was the greatest player he had ever seen.

11. Lead off hitter Roger Maris hit two home runs in his first game as a New York Yankee in 1960.

12. Rod Carew stole home seven times during his career, tying the major league record set by Pee Wee Reese.

13. George Steinbrenner paid $25 million when he bought the New York Yankees.

14. Seattle's Randy Johnson pitched his first no-hitter in 1990. At 6 feet, 10 inches he became the tallest person to ever pitch a no-no.

15. After winning his 299th game, pitcher Early "Gus" Wynn lost his next eight decisions and retired having never won No. 300.

Answers: *The American League*

1. True. The record-setting turnout was a fare-well to Cleveland Stadium. The Indians began playing in a newly constructed stadium in 1994.
2. False. George Brett did, however, single up the middle.
3. False. In 1972, Oakland owner Charlie Finley encouraged his players to grow mustaches but offered to pay $300, not $3,000. Several players gladly took Finley up on his offer. Pitcher Rollie Fingers was among them and still dons his renowned handlebar mustache today.
4. True. The back of Carlos May's White Sox uniform read "May 17."
5. True. Paul Richards called his oversized catcher's mitt "Big Bertha."
6. False. Al Rosen was the 1952 MVP. Rosen was an outstanding third baseman for the Cleveland Indians from 1947 to 1956. He led the American League with 43 HRs and 145 RBI his MVP season. It would never have happened if Rosen had taken the advice of his first manager, Elmer Yoder. Rosen first broke into baseball when he tried out with a Boston farm team in Suffolk, Va. After observing Rosen, Yoder told him that he would never make it as a baseball player. Neither Rosen nor Yoder made it to the Baseball Hall of Fame but Rosen deserves to be a member. Not only did Rosen have an outstanding baseball career, but he went on to become President of the New York Yankees and the Houston Astros. In 1985, Rosen took over as President and General Manager of the San Francisco Giants. Within two years the Giants went from worst to first in their division. Two years later they played against Oakland in the 1989 World Series. Rosen retired from the game in 1993.
7. True. In 1953, Billy Martin set an American League World Series record with 10 hits.
8. True. In 1950, Billy Martin set a record with two hits in a single inning in his first major league game. He did it against the Red Sox.
9. True. Yogi Berra's Yankees lost the 1964 World Series to the Cardinals in seven games. Soon after, Berra was fired. He was replaced by Cardinal manager Johnny Keane, who had just beaten Berra in the Series. The Yankees were under .500 Keane's first season in New York and he was fired during the 1966 season after the team started poorly. Keane never managed again.
10. False. Billy Martin said his best friend, Mickey Mantle, not Joe DiMaggio, was the greatest player he had ever seen.
11. True
12. False. It was Pete Reiser who stole home seven times, not Pee Wee Reese.

13. False. $25 million for the Yankees would have been a bargain, but George Steinbrenner paid even less, $10 million.

14. True

15. False. "Gus" Wynn won exactly 300 games during his 21-year career. He won 20 games five times and won the Cy Young Award in 1959.

A PAIGE IN BASEBALL HISTORY

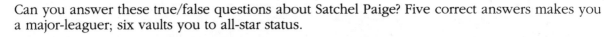

Can you answer these true/false questions about Satchel Paige? Five correct answers makes you a major-leaguer; six vaults you to all-star status.

1. Paige's baseball career stretched more than 40 years, first playing in the Negro Leagues and later for the Cleveland Indians.

2. When Paige arrived in the American League in June of 1947, he was almost 40 years old.

3. Paige was the first black player to pitch in the majors.

4. Paige rubbed goose grease on his arm the days he was scheduled to pitch.

5. On days Paige wasn't scheduled to pitch he would watch the game from a rocking chair in the bullpen.

6. Cleveland was the only major league team Paige played for.

7. Paige, like Babe Ruth, learned to pitch after being sent to reform school.

8. Paige's last pitching appearance was in September of 1965. He was over 60 years old.

9. Paige never qualified for a major league baseball pension.

Answers: A Paige In Baseball History

1. True. Paige's career lasted approximately 45 years.
2. False. Paige's true age is unknown, but when he came up in 1948 as an American League rookie he was at least 42. A birth certificate shows he was born in 1906, but there is doubt as to the certificate's authenticity because his name is misspelled on the document.
3. False. Paige was, however, the first African-American to pitch in the American League.
4. True. Paige developed a sore arm pitching in the Mexican League during the summer of 1939. His arm became so sore that he couldn't lift it over his head and doctors told Paige he would never pitch again. That Fall he signed as a first baseman and pitcher with a Kansas City Monarch team that barnstormed throughout the Northwest and Canada. Hoards of fans came out to see Paige as he painfully pitched a few innings each game. One day the pain mysteriously vanished and Paige returned to his old form.
5. True
6. False. Paige played for the Indians, Browns and Athletics.
7. True. Paige was in the Alabama Industrial School for Negro Children between the ages of 12 and 17 for shoplifting and truancy at school.
8. True. Kansas City Athletics owner Charlie Finley brought Paige back to the majors for a single game in September of 1965. He pitched the first three innings.
9. False. The Atlanta Braves hired him as a coach for the 1968 and 1969 seasons which qualified him for a pension.

MORE ABOUT SATCHEL PAIGE

How good was Satchel Paige? During the early 1930s, Paige won 17 consecutive games against barnstorming teams – professional players who put together their own traveling teams during the off-season. They would travel to small towns and play exhibitions against local competition. Some of the best matchups pitted Paige and his All-Stars against Dizzy Dean and his Major League All-Stars. In one showdown, Paige pitched a 17-inning shutout against Dean. Paige struck out Rogers Hornsby five times, and Charlie Gehringer and Jimmy Foxx three times each that day.

During another exhibition, Paige pitched six innings of no-hit baseball, striking out 16 of the 18 batters he faced.

Pitching for the Pittsburgh Crawfords, Paige won approximately 110 games during a three-year period.

Paige was certainly one of the greatest pitchers in baseball history. His success in the Negro Leagues and barnstorming circuit made him a hero to many African Americans. At the height of his career, his appearance fees pushed his annual salary as high as $50,000, a figure much higher than what he would have earned if he had been allowed to pitch in the major leagues. He toured not only in the United States, but in Canada, Mexico, Venezuela and the Dominican Republic, always drawing big crowds.

BY THE NUMBERS

Can you match the uniform numbers on the right with the appropriate all-star? Seven correct answers makes you a major-leaguer; eight vaults you to all-star status.

PLAYERS	NUMBERS
1. _____ Phil Rizzuto	41
2. _____ Willie Mays	5
3. _____ Ted Williams	1
4. _____ Lou Gehrig	4
5. _____ Mike Schmidt	20
6. _____ Hank Aaron	10
7. _____ Johnny Bench	9
8. _____ Billy Martin	24
9. _____ Tom Seaver	44

Did You Know?

In 1950, Billy Martin and Phil Rizzuto were roommates. Martin played in approximately 30 games that season while Rizzuto played every day and was on his way toward being named MVP that year. One day Rizzuto received a death threat in the mail. The writer claimed he would shoot Rizzuto during batting practice. Naturally, Rizzuto was alarmed and informed Manager Casey Stengel. When Stengel heard about the threat to his star shortstop, he had Martin and Rizzuto switch uniforms. Rizzuto wore Martin's No. 1 and Martin wore Rizzuto's No. 10. It didn't take long for Martin to insist on returning to his original number.

Answers: By the Numbers

10 = Phil Rizzuto
24 = Willie Mays
9 = Ted Williams
4 = Lou Gehrig
20 = Mike Schmidt
44 = Hank Aaron
5 = Johnny Bench
1 = Billy Martin
41 = Tom Seaver

MORE ABOUT THE AMERICAN LEAGUE

Can you answer these true/false questions about the American League? Five correct answers makes you a major-leaguer; six vaults you to all-star status.

1. Nolan Ryan came to the big leagues in 1966, but didn't make his first start in an All-Star Game until 1979 when he was pitching for the California Angels.

2. Third baseman Alan "Dirty Al" Gallagher was with the Giants and Angels during the early 1970s. His lifetime batting average was .263 with 11 HRs. His full name is Alan Mitchell Edward George Patrick Henry Gallagher.

3. As of the 1993 season, George Brett was the only American Leaguer with 300 hits, 300 home runs and 200 stolen bases.

4. At the end of the 1993 regular season, Rickey Henderson had reached the 1,100 stolen bases plateau.

5. Mickey Mantle and Eddie Murray have hit home runs from both sides of the plate in the same game on 10 or more occasions.

6. The name of the new Texas Rangers ballpark, built in Arlington Texas in 1993, is "The Ballpark."

7. Gaylord Perry won the Cy Young Award twice, both times in the American League.

8. During the 1993 season, Sparky Anderson became the second winningest manager in baseball history. Only Connie Mack has won more games.

After 21 seasons in the major leagues, George Brett retired in 1993.

Answers: More About the American League

1. True
2. True. Everyone called him "Al" for short.
3. True. George Brett is the only American Leaguer to accomplish this feat. Two National Leaguers have done it.
4. False. Rickey Henderson had only 1,095.
5. True
6. True

7. False. Gaylord Perry won a Cy Young Award, once in each league.
8. False. Sparky Anderson did manage major league teams that won more than 2,000 games, but as of the end of the 1993 season he's seventh on the all-time list.

THE WORLD SERIES

Can you answer these multiple choice questions about the World Series? Twelve correct answers makes you a major-leaguer; 15 vaults you to all-star status.

1. What Toronto Blue Jay was the MVP of the 1992 World Series?

a. Joe Carter
b. Roberto Alomar
c. Pat Borders
d. Dave Winfield

2. What relief pitcher struck out a record-setting six consecutive batters in a World Series?

a. Lee Smith
b. Rollie Fingers
c. Moe Drabowsky

3. For what achievement does Jackie Robinson hold the National League record, but not the major league record?

a. Most runs scored in a World Series
b. Most stolen bases in a World Series
c. Most World Series MVPs

4. The World Series career record of 14 stolen bases was set by what St. Louis Cardinal?

A. Vince Coleman
b. Lou Brock
c. Pepper Martin

5. What player holds the World Series record for the highest career slugging percentage (.755)? (Minimum 50 at bats required.)

a. Hank Aaron
b. Dave Henderson
c. Reggie Jackson

6. What New York Yankee holds the record of 42 RBI in World Series competition?

a. Lou Gehrig
b. Mickey Mantle
c. Hank Bauer

7. What Dodger holds the National League record of 26 RBI in World Series competition?

a. Duke Snider
b. Gil Hodges
c. Pedro Guerrero
d. Ron Cey

8. What American League player holds the record for the most home runs in World Series competition (18)?

a. Reggie Jackson
b. Babe Ruth
c. Mickey Mantle

9. Who holds the record for the most home runs in World Series competition by a National League player (11)?

a. Gil Hodges
b. Johnny Bench
c. Duke Snider

10. A pitcher was named MVP of the 1989, 1990, and 1991 World Series. Who of the following was not World Series MVP during those three years?

a. Jack Morris
b. Dave Stewart
c. Jose Rijo
d. Juan Guzman

11. What Yankee was the first American League player to hit a game-winning home run in the World Series?

a. Tommy Henrich (1949)
b. Babe Ruth (1932)
c. Joe DiMaggio (1936)

12. What New York Giant was the first National League player to hit a game-winning home run in the World Series?

a. George Kelly (1921)
b. Dusty Rhodes (1954)
c. Willie Mays (1951)

13. Who was the first to have five hits in a World Series game?

a. Billy Martin
b. Stan Musial
c. Paul Molitor

14. Who has the all-time highest World Series batting average (.418)? (Minimum 50 at bats required.)

a. Pepper Martin
b. Lou Brock
c. Hank Aaron

15. The 1993 World Series received the second-lowest viewer rating in the 35-year history of World Series television broadcasting. What World Series received the lowest rating?

a. Atlanta vs. Toronto (1992)
b. Oakland vs. San Francisco (1989)
c. Minnesota vs. St. Louis (1987)

16. What is the only team to lose three consecutive World Series?

a. Brooklyn Dodgers, 1951-1953
b. Washington Senators, 1924-26
c. New York Giants, 1911-13

17. The great New York Yankees teams of the 1930s had a lineup with what distinct nickname?

a. Murderers' Row
b. The Lumber Crew
c. The Bronx Bombers

18. The record for most runs scored by a losing team in a World Series game was set by Philadelphia in a 15-14 loss to Toronto in 1993. What team held the previous record?

a. 1954 Indians (Game 5)
b. 1975 Red Sox (Game 6)
c. 1960 Yankees (Game 7)

19. Who was pitching for Boston during the 1986 World Series when a ground ball went between the legs of first baseman Bill Buckner for an error and allowed New York to score the winning run in Game 6?

a. Joe Sambito
b. Al Nipper
c. Bob "Big Foot" Stanley

20. Two brothers played against each other in the 1964 Cardinals/Yankees World Series. Both played third base. Who were they?

a. Marv and Lee Grissom
b. Clete and Ken Boyer
c. Dolf and Doug Camilli

Answers: *The World Series*

1. c, Pat Borders
2. c, Moe Drabowsky
3. a, Runs scored (22). Eight other American Leaguers have scored more, led by Mickey Mantle (42)
4. b, Lou Brock. Incidentally, Vince Coleman has stolen six bases in seven World Series games.
5. c, Reggie Jackson. Babe Ruth is second (.744), followed by Lou Gehrig (.731). Dave Henderson is 10th (.606) and Hank Aaron 11th, (.600).
6. b, Mickey Mantle. Yogi Berra has 39, Lou Gehrig 35, Babe Ruth 33, Joe DiMaggio 30, and Hank Bauer 24.
7. a, Duke Snider. Gil Hodges had 21 and Pedro Guerrero had just 15 in postseason play. He only played in one World Series (1981) where he had two HRs and seven RBI as the Dodgers beat the Yankees in six games.
8. c, Mickey Mantle. Reggie Jackson hit 18 in the postseason but that included two World Series appearances.
9. c, Duke Snyder is fourth overall, behind Mickey Mantle, Babe Ruth and Yogi Berra.
10. d, Juan Guzman
11. a, Tommy Henrich. It came off Dodger pitcher Don Newcome in Game 1, and was the game's only run.
12. b, Dusty Rhodes. It was against Bob Lemon of the Indians in Game 1 as a pinch hitter. The Giants won the game 5-2 and the series in a sweep.
13. c, Paul Molitor. He did it as a Brewer in the 1982 Series.
14. a, Pepper Martin. The St. Louis Cardinal was nicknamed "The Wild Horse of the Osage" because of his aggressiveness. He was perhaps at his best during the 1931 World Series against the Philadelphia Athletics. In Game 1 he had three hits off the great Lefty Grove. In Game 2, he totaled two hits, two

steals and two runs in a 2-0 win. In Game 5 he had three hits, including a home run and four RBI. In Game 7 he made a game-saving catch as the Cards won the Series. Martin's World Series totals were 12 for 24 batting (.500), including four doubles, a home run, five RBI, five runs scored and five stolen bases.

15. b, Oakland/San Francisco World Series. The Series had a 16.4 rating. The 1993 Series received a 17.3 rating, down 14 percent from the 20.2 rating of the 1992 Atlanta/Toronto series.

16. c, New York Giants
17. a, Murderers' Row
18. c, 1960 Yankees. New York scored nine runs in the seventh game of the 1960 World Series, but lost 10-9 to Pittsburgh
19. c, Bob Stanley
20. b, Clete and Ken Boyer

WHAT PITCHER SAID IT?

Match the quotes with the pitcher who said them. Seven correct answers makes you a major-leaguer; nine vaults you to all-star status.

a. Sandy Koufax

b. Cy Young

c. Jim "Catfish" Hunter

d. Nolan Ryan

e. Sparky Lyle

f. Gaylord Perry

g. Dan Quisenberry

h. Satchel Paige

i. Rollie Fingers

j. Don Drysdale

1. _____ retired from baseball in September of 1993 after injuring his elbow while pitching for the Texas Rangers. Reflecting on his first major league post with the New York Mets, he said, "I had to figure out for myself what it took to win. I spent a lot of time watching (Tom) Seaver and (Jerry) Koosman...They threw strikes and pitched with confidence."

2. _____, a Hall of Fame reliever who won 114 games and saved 341 during his career, was invited to spring training in 1986 by Cincinnati Reds Manager Pete Rose with the proviso that he shave off his famous mustache because owner Marge Schott insisted her players not display any facial hair. His response to Rose was, "You tell Marge to shave her St. Bernard, and I'll shave my mustache."

3. _____, nicknamed "The Great Expectorator," said, "Three-hundred wins is nothing to spit at" in May of 1982.

4. _____, a former Dodger pitcher noted for hitting batters, recalled, "Once the manager came out to the mound and instructed me to walk a batter. I wound up hitting him instead. Why waste four pitches when one will do?"

5. _____, another former Dodger who, when asked about pitching, replied, "Pitching is the art of instilling fear by making a man flinch."

6. _____, the first black pitcher in the American League, said, "Throw strikes, home plate don't move."

7. _____, the premier Yankee reliever during the 1970s, asked, "Why pitch nine innings when you can get just as famous pitching two?"

8. _____ said, "Thank you, Peter Seitz," after being declared a free agent by an arbitrator in 1975, which allowed him to sign with the New York Yankees for $3.5 million, making him the highest paid player at the time.

9. _____, said to be a very funny man, was named American League Fireman of the Year five times with the Kansas City Royals before being released in 1988. Immediately after becoming a free agent, he signed with the St. Louis Cardinals. Manager Whitey Herzog once observed that he wasn't as funny as he had been when they were both with the Royals, to which he replied, "When you're going (nowhere), you're not as funny anymore."

10. _____, who holds the record for wins, said, "I never warmed up like most pitchers do. I'd loosen up for maybe three or four minutes. I aimed to make the batter hit the ball, and I made as few pitches as possible. That's why I was able to work every other day."

Answers: What Pitcher Said It?

1. d, Nolan Ryan
2. i, Rollie Fingers
3. f, Gaylord Perry
4. j, Don Drysdale
5. a, Sandy Koufax
6. h, Satchel Paige
7. e, Sparky Lyle
8. c, Jim Hunter went 26-2, including five no-hitters, during his high school career. He was signed by the Athletics right out of high school for the 1964 season, but was unable to play immediately because of a hunting accident. Hunter and his brother, Pete, were walking in the woods when the shotgun Pete was carrying accidentally went off and shot Jim in the foot. Doctors removed most of the buckshot and amputated the little toe on his right foot. It didn't bother his pitching because he made the A's squad in 1965 and became one of the few to reach the majors directly from high school. It was Oakland owner Charlie Finley who gave Hunter the nickname "Catfish." Finley also dubbed Hunter's teammate, Jim Grant, also a pitcher, "Mudcat" because he believed nicknames appealed to the fans.
9. g, Dan Quisenberry
10. b, Cy Young

ON THE HILL

Can you answer these multiple choice questions about pitchers? Nine correct answers makes you a major-leaguer; 11 vaults you to all-star status.

1. Who was the first American League relief pitcher to win the Cy Young Award?

a. Sparky Lyle
b. Rollie Fingers
c. Dan Quisenberry

2. Who is the only pitcher to have consecutive no-hitters?

a. Orel Hershiser
b. Allie Reynolds
c. Johnny Vander Meer

3. Nolan Ryan holds many pitching records, including the most strikeouts in a season. Whose record did Ryan break when he struck out his 383rd batter in 1973?

a. Tom Seaver
b. Sandy Koufax
c. Steve Carlton

4. Who was the first to throw two extra-inning no-hitters?

a. Dizzy Dean
b. Jim Maloney
c. Jim Bunning

5. Who was the first to have back-to-back 300 strikeout seasons?

a. Cy Young
b. Bob Feller
c. Nolan Ryan

6. What Boston pitcher, in 1876, is said to have thrown the first no-hitter?

a. Joe Borden
b. Bruce "Farmer" Miller
c. Jerry "The Banker" Havranek

7. What Boston pitcher set baseball's all-time lowest ERA of 1.01 in 1914?

a. "Smokey" Joe Wood
b. Hubert "Dutch" Leonard
c. Ernie Shore

8. Who did the New York Mets get when they traded away Nolan Ryan?

a. Joe Foy
b. Amos Otis
c. Jim Fregosi

9. Who was the first relief pitcher to be elected to the Hall of Fame?

a. Hoyt Wilhelm
b. Joe Page
c. Rollie Fingers

10. Nolan Ryan, who retired at the end of the 1993 season, struck out 5,714 batters during his career. Who was Ryan's very first strikeout victim?

a. Ron Oester
b. Pat Jarvis
c. Willie McCovey

11. Who was Nolan Ryan's victim when he broke the record for strikeouts in a season in 1973 (383)?

a. Tony Oliva
b. Rich Reese
c. Rod Carew

12. Who is the only pitcher to win the Cy Young Award and be named Rookie of the Year in the same season?

a. Tom Seaver
b. Fernando Valenzuela
c. Roger Clemens

13. What New York Yankee holds the distinction of pitching the only perfect game in the World Series?

a. Don Larsen
b. Whitey Ford
c. Allie Reynolds

14. Who was the only pitcher to be named MVP twice?

a. Vida Blue
b. Hal Newhouser
c. Robin Roberts

15. Which New York Met struck out 19 batters in a single game and set a major league record with 10 consecutive Ks?

a. Dwight Gooden
b. Nolan Ryan
c. Tom Seaver

Answers: On the Hill

1. a, Sparky Lyle did it in 1977.
2. c, Johnny Vander Meer. While pitching with the Reds in 1938, Vander Meer pitched his first no-hitter during a day game in Cincinnati. Four days later he repeated against the Dodgers in the first night game ever played at Ebbets Field.
3. b, Sandy Koufax. Koufax had held the record of 382 strikeouts in a single season until, on the last day of the 1973 season, Nolan Ryan struck out 16 Twins in 10 innings and surpassed the Koufax record by one strikeout.
4. b, Jim Maloney. In 1965, Maloney pitched 10 no-hit innings against the New York Mets, but lost 1-0 when he gave up a home run in the 11th. Later that season Maloney beat the Cubs 1-0 with a no-hitter in 10 innings.
5. c, Nolan Ryan. Ryan had back-to-back 300 strikeout seasons for the California Angels in 1972 and 1973. He made it three seasons in a row in 1974.
6. a, Joe Borden
7. b, Hubert "Dutch" Leonard
8. c, Jim Fergosi. Claiming New York City was too big for his liking, Nolan Ryan asked to

In 1993, Nolan Ryan ended his 27-year major league career as the game's all-time strikeout leader with 5,714.

be traded. The Mets dealt him to the California Angels for three players, including shortstop Fregosi.
9. a, Hoyt Wilhem
10. b, Pat Jarvis

11. b, Rich Reese
12. b, Fernando Valenzuela
13. a, Don Larsen
14. b, Hal Newhouser
15. c, Tom Seaver

HEAD-TO-HEAD AT CATCHER

Can you answer these 19 questions about three major league catchers and their 1993 seasons? The answers to questions 1-15 are found in the 1993 Box Score Comparison on the next page. Eight correct answers makes you a major-leaguer; 10 vaults you to all-star status.

a. Darren Daulton	b. Pat Borders	c. Mickey Tettleton
Philadelphia Phillies	Toronto Blue Jays	Detroit Tigers

1. Who had less than 500 at bats?

2. Who had the most at bats?

a. 105 to 119
b. 120 to 134
c. 135 to 149

3. All three had batting averages within 15 points of each other. Within what range did their averages fall?

a. .230 to .244
b. .245 to .259
c. .260 to .274

4. Who drove in the most runs?

5. Who had the fewest RBI?

6. All three were within 14 hits of each other. In what range did they fall?

7. Who had the most extra base hits?

8. Who had the most home runs?

9. Who had the fewest home runs?

10. Who scored the most runs?

11. Who scored the fewest runs?

12. Who stole the most bases?

13. Who stole the fewest bases?

14. Who made the most errors?

15. Who made the fewest errors?

16. All three were platooned early in their careers. Who platooned with John Russell?

17. Who platooned with Terry Kennedy?

18. Who was the only one released by a major league team?

19. Who did not switch to catching until his fifth season in the majors?

1993 Box Score Comparison

Player	AVG	AB	R	H	XBH	HR	RBI	S	E
a. Darren Daulton	.257	510	90	131	39	24	105	5	9
b. Pat Borders	.256	480	37	123	30	9	55	2	13
c. Mickey Tettleton	.245	522	79	128	29	32	110	3	6

Answers to questions 16-19:
16. a, Darren Daulton; 17. c, Mickey Tettleton; 18. c, Mickey Tettleton; 19. b, Pat Borders

THE AMERICAN LEAGUE (PART II)

Can you answer these true/false questions about the American League. Nine correct answers makes you a major-leaguer; 11 vaults you to all-star status.

1. George Bell, released by the Chicago White Sox at the end of the 1993 season, was the first Toronto Blue Jay to hit a grand slam home run.

2. The longest game in major league history was between Chicago and Milwaukee on May 9, 1984. It lasted eight hours and six minutes.

3. New York pitcher Ron Guidry once played the drums during a post-game Beach Boys concert in Yankee Stadium.

4. Oakland gave catcher Mickey Tettleton his outright release at the end of the 1988 season.

5. Mark McGwire took a voluntary pay cut before the 1992 season after batting a disappointing .201 with 22 HRs, 75 RBI and 116 strikeouts in 1991.

6. The tallest major league player to be named Rookie of the Year was Washington Senators outfielder Albie Pearson in 1958.

7. In December of 1966, the New York Yankees traded two-time MVP Roger Maris to the St. Louis Cardinals for infielder Charlie Smith, who was a career .239 hitter.

8. The Minnesota Twins never won a pennant when Billy Martin was the team's manager.

9. Long-time New York Yankee third base coach Frank Crosetti played third base for the Yankees from 1932-1948.

10. Seattle Mariners Manager Lou Piniella and Dave Magadan are cousins.

11. Bill Veeck, one-time owner of the St. Louis Browns, once inserted a midget into the lineup to pinch-hit as part of a promotional stunt.

12. The same Bill Veeck owned three different major league clubs, including the Chicago White Sox.

13. Bill Veeck bought and sold the Chicago White Sox twice.

14. Bill Veeck tried to buy the Minnesota Twins in 1957.

15. Goose Gossage has never been the starting pitcher in a major league game.

16. Hall of Fame pitcher Rollie Fingers lost more games than he won.

17. Roger Clemens had the first losing season in his career in 1993.

Answers: The American League (Part II)

1. False. Jesse Barfield hit the first grand slam home run for Toronto.
2. True
3. True. Ron Guidry was an excellent amateur drummer. He even kept a set of drums at Yankee Stadium.
4. True
5. True
6. False. Albie Pearson was Rookie of the Year in 1958, but at 5'5" he is the *shortest* player in major league history.
7. True. A year after getting Roger Maris, the Cardinals improved from their sixth-place finish of 1966 to World Champions. They repeated in 1968. Charlie Smith was a competent third baseman who could play shortstop if needed. An original Met, Smith led the team in 1964 with 20 HRs. At the end of the 1965 season he was part of a trade that brought former MVP Ken Boyer to New York from the Cardinals. He may be the only player in major league history to be traded for two different MVPs in consecutive seasons. Smith played for the Dodgers, Phillies, White Sox, Mets, Cardinals, Yankees and Cubs. He is one of only two people to play for both Chicago and both New York teams. Relief pitcher Dick "Dirt" Tidrow is the other.
8. False. In 1969, Billy Martin led the Twins to the division championship in his first year as their manager, and was fired shortly after losing to Baltimore in the league championship Series.
9. False. Frank Crosetti was the Yankee shortstop from 1932-1948.
10. True
11. True
12. True. Bill Veeck owned the Indians, St. Louis Browns and White Sox.
13. True
14. False. Bill Veeck did, however, attempt to buy the Detroit Tigers in 1957.
15. False. Goose Gossage was a starting pitcher for the Chicago White Sox during the 1976 season. He was 9-17 with a 3.94 ERA that year.
16. True. Rollie Fingers' lifetime record was 114-118. He was "saving" himself for the Hall of Fame.
17. True

1930s & 1940s

Can you answer these multiple choice questions about baseball in the 1930s and 1940s? Eight correct answers makes you a major-leaguer; 10 vaults you to all-star status.

1. When Jackie Robinson came to the plate on opening day at Ebbets Field in 1947 as a member of the Brooklyn Dodgers, who threw the historical first pitch to the first black player in major-league history?

a. Johnny Sain
b. Warren Spahn
c. Vern Bickford

2. What position did Jackie Robinson play in his first major-league game?

a. shortstop
b. first base
c. second base
d. third base

3. How many hits did Jackie Robinson get in his first major-league game?

a. 0
b. 2
c. 3

4. What relief pitcher led the National League in appearances three times during the first half of the 1940s, including a major-league record 70 appearances in 1943?

a. Ivy Andrews
b. Al Smith
c. Ace Adams

5. What National Leaguer and eventual Hall-of-Famer was sold to the New York Yankees in 1949, where, after considered to be in the twilight of is career, he became a premier pinch-hitter through five straight New York championship seasons?

a. Johnny Mize
b. Tommy Henrich
c. Charlie Keller

6. What National Leaguer became the first "pure" relief pitcher to be chosen for the All-Star game in 1938?

a. Ace Adams
b. Mace Brown
c. Dick Coffman

7. Who was pitching when Babe Ruth allegedly made his immortal gesture to center field, only to hit a home run to that spot on the next pitch in the 1932 World Series?

a. Lon Warneke
b. Jakie May
c. Charlie Root

8. Who was New York's opponent in that 1932 World Series?

a. New York Giants
b. St. Louis Cardinals
c. Chicago Cubs

9. The 1945 Washington Senators had a pitcher with one leg. Who was he?

a. Eddie Klieman
b. Bert Shepard
c. Les Mueller

10. Who was the first catcher to win two batting titles (1938 and 1942)?

a. Ernie Lombardi
b. Bill Dickey
c. Mickey Owen

11. Who was named National League MVP three times in the 1940s ('43, '46 and '48)?

a. Marty Marion
b. Stan Musial
c. Bob Elliott

12. Who was named American League MVP three times in the 1930s (1932-33 and '38)?

a. Hank Greenberg
b. Jimmie Foxx
c. Charlie Gehringer

13. What New York Giant pitcher was a unanimous choice for the MVP in 1936?

a. Freddie Fitzsimmons
b. Hal Schumacher
c. Carl Hubbell

Answers: 1930s & 1940s

1. a, A popular cliche in the 1940s that referred to a struggling Boston Braves' pitching staff was "Spahn and Sain and pray for rain." Though clever, it was misleading. Another pitcher on the staff was Vern Bickford, who went 11-5 for the National League champion Braves of 1948. In 1950, he led the league in complete games (27), innings pitched (312) and won 19 games, including a no-hitter against the Dodgers. Unfortunately, he broke a finger on his pitching hand in 1951 and was forced to retire at age 31.

2. b, first base
3. a, 0
4. c, Ace Adams is scarcely remembered because his successes occurred during World War II. Adams got his start in professional baseball playing in the Industrial League for the El Rey Brewery in San Francisco, California. His payroll job was as a clock-winder, but his real value to the company was as its starting pitcher. Industrial Leagues were made up of teams sponsored by large companies. Some players were regular employees and others, like Adams, were "ringers." Adams' secret to success was his curveball. He would mix rosin and tobacco juice in his mouth and then lick his fingers (still legal in those days). The result was a wicked curve. In 1946, Adams was offered $50,000 a year to play in the newly-formed Mexican League. He quickly accepted and after one year Adams retired to Albany, Georgia, and opened Ace's Oyster Bar, which still exists today.

5. a, Johnny Mize
6. b, Pirate reliever Mace Brown was the first pitcher to be referred to as "Fireman" be-

79

cause he often hung around a neighbor-hood firehouse, socializing and playing horseshoes. A local sportswriter thought it would be clever to take a picture of Brown wearing a fireman's hat. Relief pitchers have been compared to firemen ever since because of their reputation for coming to the rescue when the game is on the line. Brown led the National League relievers in appearances in 1937 and 1938, and again in 1943 with Boston.

7. c, Charlie Root
8. c, Chicago Cubs
9. b, Bert Shepard. Baseball lost a significant portion of its talent pool to World War II,

thus increasing the chances of players like Shepard, who had a wooden leg, of reaching the majors. His stay with the Senators was brief.

10. a, During a game in 1943 between the New York Giants and Pittsburgh, New York catcher Ernie Lombardi was catching for pitcher Ace Adams. One particular Adams fastball sailed outside. Rather than reach across his body to try and catch the ball, Lombardi caught the ball with his bare hand.

11. b, Stan Musial
12. b, Jimmie Foxx
13. c, Carl Hubbell

WORLD SERIES GAME-WINNING HOME RUNS

Can you answer these multiple choice questions about World Series game-winning home runs? Only one correct answer makes you a major-leaguer; two vaults you to all-star status.

1. Off of what New York Yankee did New York Giant center fielder Casey Stengel hit a game-winning home run in Game 3 of the 1923 World Series?

a. Sad Sam Jones
b. Bullet Joe Bush
c. Herb Pennock

2. Off of what Brooklyn Dodger did New York Yankee second baseman Tommy Henrich hit a game-winning home run in the bottom of the ninth inning of Game 1 during the 1949 World Series?

a. Preacher Roe
b. Rex Barney
c. Don Newcome

3. Off of what Los Angeles Dodger did Baltimore Oriole center fielder Paul Plair hit a game-winning home run in Game 3 of the 1966 World Series?

a. Claude Osteen
b. Ron Perranoski
c. Phil Regan

4. Off of what Los Angeles Dodger did Baltimore Oriole right fielder Frank Robinson hit a game-winning home run in Game 4 of the 1966 World Series?

a. Jim Brewer
b. Don Drysdale
c. Bob Miller

1993 World Series

Philadelphia closer Mitch Williams didn't lead the National League in saves in 1993 but his 43 saves were a major factor in the Phillies winning the pennant. That's why Philadelphia fans were shocked when Toronto's Joe Carter hit a game-winning, two-run home run with his team trailing by a run in the bottom of the ninth inning in Game 6. That blast won the Series for the Blue Jays and landed Williams in Houston via the trading block.

The 1993 World Series was only the second in history to end with a home run. The other was the 1960 Series between the Pirates and Yankees when Pittsburgh's Bill Mazeroski hit a solo homer off Ralph Terry in the bottom of the ninth.

During the Williams/Carter ninth-inning faceoff Williams shook off the initial sign given him by Phillies catcher Darren Daulton. We'll never know what might have been if Williams had thrown the pitch Daulton called for.

Perhaps Williams threw the pitch Daulton intended. The duo often played a psychological game with batters. Williams, pretending to shake off a sign, would, in fact, throw the pitch called for. The intent was to make the batter second guess himself about what pitch to expect.

The infamous pitch to Carter was a good one and placed in the correct location. Carter should be commended for getting the job done. After all, Carter is one of the better hitters in baseball. But how will Williams be affected by the historic at bat? Hopefully he will fare better than former California Angels pitcher Donnie Moore.

Moore's life was shattered in 1986 when he served a pitch to Boston's Dave Henderson during Game 5 of the American League Championship Series. The drama began in the ninth with the Angels leading 5-2. The Red Sox opened with a hit and an out, followed by a Don Baylor home run to left field. After Boston recorded its second out, Red Sox catcher Rich Gedman was hit by a pitch, which brought Henderson to the plate with his team down by a run. Angel Manager Gene Mauch called for his closer (Moore) to pitch to Henderson.

The first pitch was a called strike and the second made the outfielder swing and miss at a poor pitch. The next two pitches were outside the strike zone, followed by two foul balls. The seventh pitch was a split-fingered fast ball that hung over the plate, and Henderson hammered it over the left field wall. The Red Sox went on to win the game in 11 innings thanks to a Henderson sacrifice fly that drove in the winning run. The Red Sox won the next two games and the series, and met the New York Mets in the World Series.

Moore blamed himself for losing the pivotal game. He told reporters afterward, "I blew it (the game)...I'll think about that until the day I die."

For all practical purposes, Moore's career ended that day. He continued to pitch for the Angels for the remainder of his three-year contract, but management released him in 1988 because of his inability to save games.

In 1989, he surfaced with the Omaha (Neb.) Royals at the Triple A level but continued to struggle, and was released mid-way through the season.

Moore's anguish eventually cost him his life. During an argument with his wife, he shot her three times. Their 17-year-old daughter drove her mother to the hospital as Moore stayed behind and, with his 10-year-old son as witness, shot himself in the head. Moore's wife survived without serious complications.

Moore became obsessed with his failure to retire Henderson in Game 5 of the 1986 American League Championship Series. He blamed himself for Henderson's home run and for his team's failure to get to the World Series. That obsession created a climate of failure. His career ended, his marriage crumbled, and it climaxed with him taking his own life. Unfortunately, baseball was more than a game for Moore.

Unlike Moore, Terry put his 1960 World Series defeat behind him and went on to become a successful pitcher. In 1961, he was 16-3. A year later he led the American League with 23 wins and pitched brilliantly in the World Series as the Yankees won in seven games over the San Francisco Giants. Terry won twice during that Series, including a 1-0 victory in Game 7 which earned him World Series MVP honors.

Answers: World Series Game-Winning Home Runs

1. a, Sad Sam Jones
2. c, Don Newcome
3. a, Claude Osteen
4. b, Don Drysdale. Baltimore swept Los Angeles 4-0 in the 1966 World Series. The Dodgers lost Games 3 and 4, 1-0, and were also shut out in Game 2. Moe Drabowsky won the first game 5-2 in relief of Dave McNally; Jim Palmer won Game 2, 6-0; Wally Bunker won Game 3 and McNally the finale. He was the only pitcher without a 0.00 ERA (1.59).

MIXING BUSINESS WITH BASEBALL

Many of baseball's team owners also operate other businesses. Can you match the teams with the other business its owner oversees? Six correct answers makes you a major-leaguer; eight vaults you to all-star status.

TEAMS

1. _____ Detroit Tigers

2. _____ St. Louis Cardinals

3. _____ New York Mets

4. _____ Montreal Expos

5. _____ New York Yankees

6. _____ San Diego Padres

7. _____ Seattle Mariners

8. _____ Atlanta Braves

9. _____ Chicago Cubs

CHOICES

a. Budweiser Beer

b. American Shipbuilding Company

c. Nintendo

d. Wrigley's Chewing Gum

e. Turner Broadcasting System

f. McDonald's

g. Little Caesar's Pizza

h. Doubleday Book Publishers

i. Seagram Liquors

Answers: Mixing Business with Baseball

1. g, Little Caesar's Pizza
2. a, Budweiser Beer
3. h, Doubleday Book Publishers
4. i, Seagram Liquors
5. b, American Shipbuilding Company

6. f, McDonald's
7. c, Nintendo
8. e, Turner Broadcasting System
9. d, Wrigley's Chewing Gum

OWNERS

Can you match the teams with their principal owner? Six correct answers makes you a major-leaguer; eight vaults you to all-star status.

TEAMS

1. _____ Florida Marlins

2. _____ Cincinnati Reds

3. _____ San Francisco Giants

4. _____ Pittsburgh Pirates

5. _____ Boston Red Sox

6. _____ California Angels

7. _____ Texas Rangers

8. _____ Baltimore Orioles

9. _____ Philadelphia Phillies

CHOICES

a. George Bush, Jr.

b. Bill Giles

c. Douglas Danforth

d. Haywood Sullivan

e. Marge Schott

f. Peter Angelo

g. H. Wayne Huizenga

h. Jackie Autry

i. Peter McGowan

Answers: Owners

1. g, H. Wayne Huizenga
2. e, Marge Schott
3. i, Peter McGowan
4. c, Douglas Danforth
5. d, Haywood Sullivan

6. h, Jackie Autry
7. a, George Bush, Jr.
8. f, Peter Angelo
9. b, Bill Giles

BY THE NUMBERS

Each year the Elias Sports Bureau produces a statistical analysis of all major league baseball players for the players association and Major League Baseball. The purpose of the analysis is to determine which players fall within various classifications. Based on a player's prior performance, the Elias Sports Bureau will determine if he is a Type A player (top 30 percent), a Type B player (top 50 percent but not in the upper 30 percent) or a Type C player (lower 50 percent). Teams that sign free agents ranked as either Type A or B players must compensate the teams they came from. The club that loses a Type A player is entitled to two Amateur Draft selections from the player's new team. A club that loses a Type B player gets one selection in the Amateur Draft.

According to the statistical analysis produced at the conclusion of the 1993 season by the Elias Sports Bureau, which player in each category is ranked the highest at his position? Twelve correct answers makes you a major-leaguer; 15 vaults you to all-star status.

AMERICAN LEAGUE

1. Designated hitter

a. Danny Tartabull (Yankees)
b. Paul Molitor (Blue Jays)

2. Catcher

a. Chris Hoiles (Orioles)
b. Mickey Tettleton (Tigers)

3. First base

a. Frank Thomas (White Sox)
b. Don Mattingly (Yankees)

4. Second base

a. Carlos Baerga (Indians)
b. Roberto Alomar (Blue Jays)

5. Third base

a. Kevin Seitzer (Brewers)
b. Robin Ventura (White Sox)

6. Shortstop

a. Tony Fernandez (Blue Jays)
b. Cal Ripken (Orioles)

7. Outfielders

a. Kirby Puckett (Twins)
b. Ken Griffey, Jr. (Mariners)

8. Starting pitchers

a. Jack McDowell (White Sox)
b. Juan Guzman (Blue Jays)

9. Relievers

a. Tom Hanke (Rangers)
b. Duane Ward (Blue Jays)

NATIONAL LEAGUE

1. Starting pitchers

a. Bill Swift (Giants)
b. Greg Maddux (Braves)

2. Relievers

a. Rod Beck (Giants)
b. Bryan Harvey (Marlins)

3. Outfielders

a. Barry Bonds (Giants)
b. Len Dykstra (Phillies)

4. Catchers (choose two)

a. Darren Daulton (Phillies)
b. Rick Wilkins (Cubs)
c. Mike Piazza (Dodgers)

5. First base (choose two)

a. John Kruk (Phillies)
b. Mark Grace (Cubs)
c. Fred McGriff (Braves)

6. Second base

a. Bip Roberts (Reds)
b. Ryne Sandberg (Cubs)

7. Third base

a. Terry Pendleton (Braves)
b. Charlie Hayes (Rockies)

8. Shortstop

a. Barry Larkin (Reds)
b. Jay Bell (Pirates)

Answers: *By the Numbers*

AMERICAN LEAGUE

1. b, Paul Molitor
2. a, Chris Hoiles
3. a, Frank Thomas
4. b, Roberto Alomar
5. b, Robin Ventura
6. a, Tony Fernandez
7. b, Ken Griffey, Jr.
8. a, Jack McDowell
9. b, Duane Ward

NATIONAL LEAGUE

1. b, Greg Maddux
2. a, Rod Beck
3. a, Barry Bonds
4. a,b, Darren Daulton, Rick Wilkins
5. b,c, Mark Grace, Fred McGriff
6. b, Ryne Sandberg
7. a, Terry Pendleton
8. a, Barry Larkin

ANCIENT HISTORY: BASEBALL UP TO 1930

Can you answer these multiple choice questions about the major leagues prior to 1930? Eight correct answers makes you a major-leaguer; 11 vaults you to all-star status.

1. Who is credited with throwing the first spitball?

a. Candy Cummings
b. Bobby Matthews
c. Charles "Old Hoss" Radbourn

2. Who had the most hits among pre-20th century major-leaguers?

a. Hugh Duffy
b. Roger Connor
c. Cap Anson

3. Who recorded the most hits (1,950) during the first decade of the 20th century (1900-1909)?

a. Honus Wagner
b. Sam Crawford
c. Nap Lajoie

4. Ty Cobb has baseball's highest lifetime batting average (.367). What National League player is No. 2?

a. Frankie Frisch
b. Honus Wagner
c. Rogers Hornsby

5. Who holds the American League's second-best lifetime batting average, behind Ty Cobb?

a. Tris Speaker
b. "Shoeless" Joe Jackson
c. George Sisler

6. True or false: Hockey star Wayne Gretzky and Los Angeles Kings owner Bruce McNall paid $51,000 for a 1910 Honus Wagner baseball card.

7. True or false: Ty Cobb was the first baseball player to earn $1 million.

8. Some of baseball's greatest hitters have used replicas of "Black Betsy," the name given to the bat of what legendary hitter?

a. Ty Cobb
b. Babe Ruth
c. "Shoeless" Joe Jackson

9. Which current major league team is the oldest continuously active club?

a. Braves
b. Reds
c. Cubs

10. Who had the most hits (2,085) in the 1920s?

a. Harry Heilmann
b. Sam Rice
c. Rogers Hornsby

11. True or false: "Candy" Cummings is credited for developing the curveball.

12. True or false: Albert Spalding, founder of Spalding Sporting Goods, never played baseball.

13. True or false: Hall of Fame outfielder Sam Rice never hit below .293 during his 20-year major league career, and batted .349 at age 40.

14. True or false: Sam Rice hit 340 home runs during his career.

15. True or false: Ty Cobb was known as "The Meanest Man In Baseball."

Answers: Ancient History: Baseball up to 1930

1. c, Bobby Mathews. While only 16-years old and still pitching as an amateur, Mathews was credited with throwing the first spitball. At age 20, Mathews was the winning pitcher in the first professional baseball game as Fort Wayne defeated Cleveland 2-0 in the newly formed National Association. The National Association was the predecessor to the present-day National League. Mathews is the only pitcher in baseball history to win more than 100 games as a pitcher in three different leagues (National Association, National League and American Association).

   Candy Cummings appeared in 245 games between 1866-77, posting a 146-92 record. He played for such teams as the Brooklyn Excelsiors, the Lord Baltimores and the Hartford Dark Blues. A plaque in the Baseball Hall of Fame honoring Charles "Old Hoss" Radbourn describes him as "the greatest of all 19th century pitchers." Playing for such teams as the Buffalo Bisons, the Providence Grays and the Boston Beaneaters, Radbourn was 311-194 with a 2.67 ERA.

2. c, Cap Anson. Anson is the only pre-1900 baseball player to have more than 3,000 hits. Roger Connor was second with 2,480, followed by Hugh Duffy's 2,100.

3. a, Honus Wagner. Wagner's career extended from 1897-1917. He led the league in hitting seven times and RBI four times.

4. c, Rogers Hornsby. Hornsby's lifetime batting average was .358, tops on the all-time National League list and second overall only to Ty Cobb. Hornsby was the league's MVP twice and batting champ seven times.

5. b, "Shoeless" Joe Jackson. Jackson's lifetime batting average was .356, second-best in American League history and third overall behind Ty Cobb and Rogers Hornsby. Tris Speaker and George Sisler hit .344 and .340, respectively. What an outfield that would make. Jackson was one of the greatest hitters of all time. Unfortunately, his career came to a premature end in 1920, a year after the "Black Sox" scandal when it was discovered that members of the Chicago White Sox had fixed games during the 1919 World Series against Cincinnati. Jackson and seven of his teammates were banned from baseball by Commissioner Judge Kenesaw Landis.

   It's believed that Jackson continued to play in other leagues under assumed names, but that has never been verified. It is also believed that Jackson was illiterate, unable to read and write. He could sign his name, however, but generally put off fans by asking them to come back another time when they asked for his autograph. Jackson sometimes gave away autographed baseballs that his wife privately signed for him. There are only a handful of Jackson's authentic signatures known to exist. One is on a lease he signed in 1936. The lease sold for $23,000 at an auction in New York City in 1991.

   Another Jackson signature is on his will. He died in 1951, leaving his estate and possessions to his wife. The American Heart Association and American Cancer Society were named the beneficiaries of the Jackson estate when she died in 1959. A legal battle was waged for possession of the original Jackson will in 1993 by the charities. They filed a lawsuit against Greenville (S.C.) County and the Greenville County Probate Court, who have possession of the will. The charities claim Jackson's will was the personal property of his wife and because she left all of her possessions to the charities in her will, then Jackson's will should be the property of the charities.

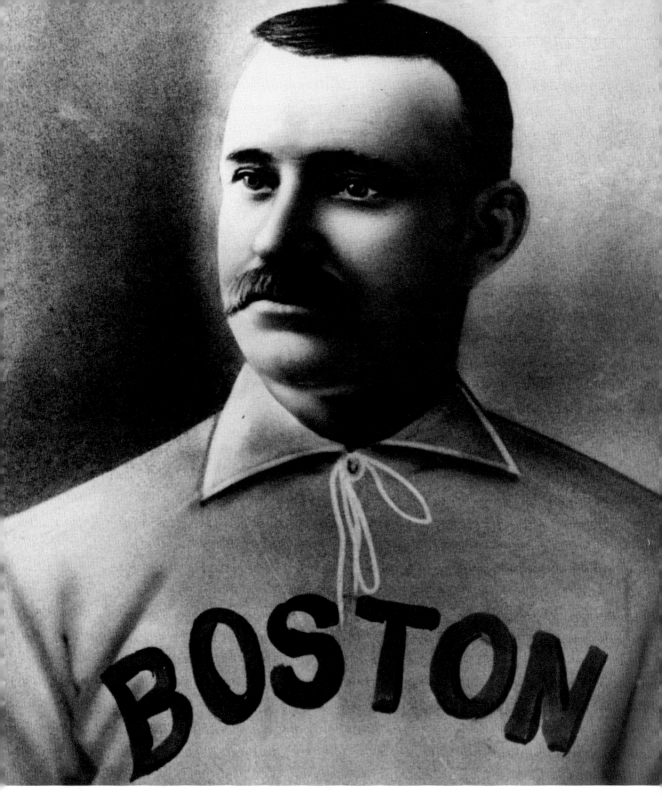

A plaque in the Baseball Hall of Fame honoring Charles "Old Hoss" Radbourn describes him as "the greatest of all 19th century pitchers." Playing for such teams as the Buffalo Bisons, the Providence Grays and the Boston Beaneaters, Radbourn was 311-194 with a 2.67 ERA.

The American Heart Association and the American Cancer Society want the courts to turn over Jackson's will to them so they can sell it and use the proceeds for medical research. The South Carolina Surpreme Court refused to hand over the will because the law states wills must be kept by the probate court for 75 years. There's little doubt the will would sell for several thousand dollars at auction.

Jackson was born in Pickens County, South Carolina in 1889 and named Joseph Jefferson Jackson. After being banned from baseball, he returned to his hometown of Greenville, S.C., where he ran a liquor store until he died. Despite his involvement in the 1919 World Series scandal, Jackson was well-liked and respected. In fact, autograph seekers, knowing of Jackson's literacy problem, kept their distance so as not to embarrass him. Following his permanent suspension, Jackson denied having participated in the Black Sox scandal, pointing to his .375 batting average during the Series. But when called to testify before the grand jury formed to investigate the case in 1920, he said "When a Cincinnati player would bat a ball out in my territory (left field) I'd muff it if I could."

6. False, Wayne Gretzky and Bruce McNall paid $451,000 for the card, not $51,000.
7. True, Ty Cobb was the first millionaire baseball player, but he didn't make the money playing baseball. Cobb's fortune came from wise stock market investments. The biggest was the purchase of 20,000 shares of Coca Cola stock.
8. c, "Shoeless" Joe Jackson
9. a, Braves. The Braves began playing in 1871 in the National Association, but they called themselves the Boston Red Stockings. Later, Boston Manager Harry Wright helped organize the Cincinnati Red Stockings. In 1876 both teams were members of the original National League. The Boston team adopted several names early in its existance, answering to Beaneaters, Braves, and Bees, before returning to the Braves moniker. The organization moved to Atlanta in 1966 after spending 13 years in Milwaukee.

Braves Owner Ted Turner purchased the failing franchise in 1976. About the same time, Turner created the Turner Broadcasting System (TBS) and began broadcasting Braves games throughout the country. He tried managing the team in the late 1970s, but it lasted one game because National League President Chub Feeney ordered him out of the dugout. Feeney said, other than being an owner, Turner had no baseball qualifications. In addition to the Braves and TBS, Turner owns the Atlanta Hawks of the National Basketball Association.

10. c, Rogers Hornsby. Hornsby had 2,085 hits in the 1920s. Sam Rice had 2,010 and Harry Heilmann, 1,924.
11. True
12. False, Albert Spalding was a major league pitcher who compiled a 255-69 record. He opened a sporting goods store with his brother, J. Walter Spalding, after retiring from baseball in 1876.
13. True
14. False, Sam Rice hit 34 home runs, not 340. Twenty-one of those round-trippers were of the inside-the-park variety.
15. True, Ty Cobb would often sit in the dugout and sharpen his spikes while the other team took infield practice.

MANAGERS AND WHERE THEY PLAYED

Can you match the baseball managers with the appropriate description about their playing days? Seven correct answers makes you a major-leaguer; eight vaults you to all-star status.

a. Butch Hobson

b. Lou Pinella

c. Tony LaRussa

d. Jim Leland

e. Tommy Lasorda

f. Dusty Baker

g. Davey Johnson

h. Hal McRae

i. Don Baylor

j. Cito Gaston

1. This former pitcher was at his best in the minors. He was 98-49 with the Dodgers' Triple A affiliate. That team won five International League championships when he was a starter. He never won a game in the majors, but tied a major league record in 1955 when he threw three wild pitches in one inning.

_____

2. This former catcher never played in the major leagues. In fact, he never played in a league higher than Double A. He was with the Tiger organization as a player from 1964 to 1969 before he started coaching.

_____

3. This former first baseman, outfielder and designated hitter had an outstanding playing career. He was named MVP in 1979 and hit 338 career home runs. He played on seven different division winners and appeared in the World Series his last three years – each time with a different team.

_____

4. This former second baseman was a three-time Gold Glove winner for the Baltimore Orioles in the late 1960s and early 1970s. He set the single-season record for home runs by a second baseman (43) in 1973 with the Braves.

_____

5. This former third baseman was a better hitter than fielder. While playing with the Red Sox, he set single season team records at his position with 30 HRs and 112 RBI in 1977. In 1978 he made 43 errors and had a fielding percentage of .899, the lowest in more than 60 years.

_____

6. This former shortstop and second baseman's major league career consisted of just 132 games with the Athletics, Braves and Cubs. Lifetime he hit .199 with no home runs and only seven RBI. He did a lot better, however, as a major league manager. In his first season, 1983, he managed the Chicago White Sox to the American League Western Division title.

_____

7. This former outfielder was a longtime friend of Los Angeles Dodger Manager Tommy Lasorda. He also played for Lasorda for eight years. They remain close friends today despite the fact they currently manage for different teams within the same division.

_____

8. This former outfielder was originally with the Braves but was taken by San Diego in the 1968 expansion draft. His best season was 1970, when he hit .318 with 29 HRs and 93 RBI.

_____

9. This former outfielder and designated hitter played for four different teams, and through 1993 has managed in three different cities. He was the Royals' Rookie of the Year in 1969 and hit .291 with 102 HRs and 766 RBI in 1,747 career games. The majority of his career (11 years) was spent with the New York Yankees but he seems happiest managing elsewhere.

_____

10. This career designated hitter came up with the Royals as an outfielder in 1968, but broke his leg in four places playing in Puerto Rico that winter. As a result, most of his career was spent as a DH. He hit over .300 six times, but never led the league in batting.

_____

Answers: Managers and Where They Played

1. e, Tommy Lasorda
2. d, Jim Leland
3. i, Don Baylor
4. g, Davey Johnson
5. a, Butch Hobson
6. c, Tony LaRussa is the only major league manager to have a law degree.
7. f, Dusty Baker
8. j, Cito Gaston became the first black manager to reach the postseason when he was named manager of the Toronto Blue Jays during the 1989 season.
9. b, Lou Pinella

10. h, In the last game of the 1976 season, Hal McRae and teammate George Brett were nearly even in the race for the batting title. In his last at bat, Brett hit a fly ball that Minnesota outfielder Steve Braun misplayed and resulted in an inside-the-park home run. It turned out to be the difference for Brett, who edged McRae for the batting title, .333 to .332. McRae and others said later they believed Braun deliberately misplayed the ball so McRae, who is black, would not win the title. Nothing ever came of the accusation.

CLASS OF '93

Can you answer these multiple choice questions about the 1993 season? Twelve correct answers makes you a major-leaguer; 15 vaults you to all-star status.

AMERICAN LEAGUE

1. What pitcher led the league with 308 strikeouts?

a. Randy Johnson
b. Kevin Appier
c. Chuck Finley

2. What pitcher was runner-up for most strikeouts with 196?

a. Juan Guzman
b. Mark Langston
c. David Cone

3. Who led the league with 129 RBI?

a. Albert Belle
b. Juan Gonzales
c. Joe Carter

4. Who was second in RBI with 128?
a. Carlos Baerga
b. Cecil Fielder
c. Frank Thomas
d. Ellis Burks

5. Who led the league with 211 hits?

a. Mike Greenwell
b. Paul Molitor
c. Kenny Lofton
d. Tim Salmon

6. Two players totalled 200 hits in 1993, tying for second place in the league. Both are listed below. Who doesn't belong?

a. Roberto Alomar
b. John Olerud
c. Carlos Baerga

7. Which New York Yankee no-hit Cleveland on September 4, 1993 in Yankee Stadium?

a. Jimmy Key
b. Melido Perez
c. Jim Abbott
d. Bob Wickman

8. What pitcher had the best winning percentage?

a. Juan Guzman
b. Randy Johnson
c. Jimmy Key

9. Who was paid $7.2 million in 1993, the highest salary in the American League and second overall?

a. Ken Griffey, Jr.
b. Roger Clemens
c. Cecil Fielder

10. Who was Rookie of the Year?

a. Aaron Sele
b. Tim Salmon
c. Jason Bere

NATIONAL LEAGUE

11. Who was Rookie of the Year?

a. Chuck Carr
b. Greg McMichael
c. Mike Piazza

12. Who led the league with 194 hits?

a. Lenny Dykstra
b. Marquis Grissom
c. Gregg Jeffries

13. Who was the league's second leading hitter with 193 hits?

a. Matt Williams
b. Mark Grace
c. Ron Gant

14. The Atlanta Braves had two 20-game winners for the first time since 1959. Which of the following Braves pitchers did not win 20 games in 1993?

a. Steve Avery
b. Tom Glavine
c. Greg Maddux

15. Who was the highest paid player in baseball in 1993?

a. Barry Bonds
b. Ryne Sandberg
c. Greg Maddux

16. Who was voted National League Manager of the Year by the Baseball Writers Association?

a. Felipe Alou
b. Dusty Baker
c. Jim Fregosi

17. Who led the major leagues in game-winning hits with 19?

a. Brett Butler
b. Ron Gant
c. Barry Bonds

18. Two Colorado Rockies each set an expansion team single season record by driving in 98 runs. Both are listed below. Who doesn't belong?

a. Daryl Boston
b. Andres Galarraga
c. Charlie Hayes

19. Which manager was runner-up as 1993 National League Manager of the Year?

a. Jim Fregosi
b. Bobby Cox
c. Don Baylor

20. What National Leaguer led the league in doubles?

a. Bernard Gilkey
b. Tony Gwynn
c. Charlie Hayes

21. Who had the highest slugging percentage?

a. Eddie Murray
b. Andres Galarraga
c. Barry Bonds

In 1993, Mike Piazza was the 13th Los Angeles Dodger voted National League Rookie of the Year. He was the Dodgers' 62nd-round pick in the 1988 draft.

Answers: Class of '93 (Part I)

1. a, Randy Johnson
2. b, Mark Langston
3. a, Albert Bell
4. c, Frank Thomas
5. b, Paul Molitor
6. a, Roberto Alomar
7. c, Jim Abbot
8. a, Juan Guzman
9. c, Cecil Fielder
10. b, Not only was Tim Salmon 1993 American League Rookie of the Year, he was also the Minor League Rookie of the Year a year earlier.
11. c, Mike Piazza was the 13th Dodger voted National League Rookie of the Year in the award's 46-year history. He was Los Angeles' 62nd-round pick in the 1988 Amateur Draft.
12. a, Lenny Dykstra
13. b, Mark Grace

14. a, Steve Avery
15. a, Barry Bonds
16. b, Dusty Baker was hired in December of 1992, shortly after new owners took control of the organization. He replaced longtime Giant Manager Roger Craig and the Giants responded by winning 103 games, one game behind Atlanta. It was the first time a team had won more than 100 games and not won the division since the 1954 Yankees finished second to Cleveland.
17. b, Ron Gant
18. a, Daryl Boston
19. a, Jim Fregosi
20. c, When Charlie Hayes led the National League in doubles for the Colorado Rockies, he became the first expansion player to lead the league in that category in baseball history.
21. c, Barry Bonds

BASEBALL BRAINTRUSTS

Using the names provided, identify the general manager and manager for the following major league teams. Eight correct answers makes you a major-leaguer; 10 vaults you to all-star status.

AMERICAN LEAGUE

a. Sandy Alderson

b. Roland Hemon

c. Hal McRae

d. Lou Piniella

e. Andy MacPhail

f. Johnny Oates

g. Ron Schueler

h. Tony LaRussa

i. Tom Kelly

j. Woody Woodward

k. Herk Robinson

l. Gene Lamont

Team	General Manager	Manager
1. Minnesota	_____	_____
2. Seattle	_____	_____
3. Oakland	_____	_____
4. Kansas City	_____	_____
5. Baltimore	_____	_____
6. Chicago	_____	_____

NATIONAL LEAGUE

a. Dusty Baker   e. Jim Leland   i. Ted Simmons

b. Bob Gebhard   f. Dallas Green   j. Davey Johnson

c. Jim Bowden   g. Joe McIlvaine   k. Bob Quinn

d. John Schuerholz   h. Don Baylor   l. Bobby Cox

Team	General Manager	Manager
7. Colorado	_____	_____
8. Pittsburgh	_____	_____
9. Cincinnati	_____	_____
10. Atlanta	_____	_____
11. San Francisco	_____	_____
12. New York	_____	_____

Answers: Baseball Braintrusts

AMERICAN LEAGUE
1. e,i, Andy MacPhail, Tom Kelly
2. j,d, Woody Woodward, Lou Pinella
3. a,h, Sandy Alderson, Tony LaRussa
4. k,c, Herk Robinson, Hal McRae
5. b,f, Roland Hemon, Johnny Oates
6. g,l, Ron Schueler, Gene Lamont

NATIONAL LEAGUE
7. b,h, Bob Gebhard, Don Baylor
8. i,e, Ted Simmons, Jim Leland
9. c,j, Jim Bowden, Davey Johnson
10. d,l, John Schuerholz, Bobby Cox
11. k,a, Bob Quinn, Dusty Baker
12. g,f, Joe McIlvaine, Dallas Green

GOING TO ALL FIELDS

Can you answer these 18 true/false questions? Twelve correct answers makes you a major-leaguer; 15 vaults you to all-star status.

1. Baseball broadcaster and former catcher Tim McCarver's playing career spanned four decades.

2. Lou Piniella came up with the Kansas City Royals in 1970 as a second baseman.

3. Of the eight members of the 1919 Chicago White Sox who admitted to fixing the World Series, only three were found guilty.

4. The poem "Casey at the Bat" was written by Robert Louis Stevenson.

5. On July 17, 1990, Boston became the first team in history to be victimized by two triple plays in the same game.

6. Former Yankee first baseman Bill Skowron was nicknamed "Moose" because he claimed to have shot a moose on a hunting trip and then carry it out of the forest single-handedly.

7. Babe Ruth began his baseball career with the Baltimore Orioles.

8. Judge Kenesaw Landis was baseball's first commissioner.

9. Ken Griffey and his son, Ken Griffey, Jr., were the first father/son duo to play in the majors at the same time.

10. Ken Griffey and his son, Ken Griffey, Jr., played for the Seattle Mariners at the same time.

11. Teams named the New York Mets and Houston Astros joined the National League as expansion teams in 1962.

12. In 1931, a woman named Jackie Mitchell struck out Babe Ruth and Lou Gehrig on six straight pitches during an exhibition game in Chattanooga, Tenn.

13. Rusty Staub holds the all-time record for pinch-hits.

14. A total of 2,074 home runs were hit in the American League in 1993, a new league record.

15. The rules for the first organized baseball game were coordinated in 1845 by Abner Doubleday.

16. The first night game in major league history was played on May 24, 1935 between Cincinnati and Philadelphia.

17. More than 70 million people attended major league baseball games in 1993.

Answers: Going to all Fields

1. True, Tim McCarver came up with the Cardinals in 1959 at the age of 17. He finished his career in Philadelphia in 1980. His first and last seasons were extremely short, however. McCarver only played in eight games in 1959, and in just six in 1980.
2. False, Lou Piniella came up in 1968 with the Cleveland Indians. His manager, Birdie Tebbetts, tried unsuccessfully to convert Pinella from an outfielder to a catcher. In 1969, Pinella was drafted by the Seattle Pilots in the expansion draft, but was soon traded to the Royals where he became Rookie of the Year. In 1993, he went back to Seattle as manager of the Mariners.
3. False, No one tried in the "Black Sox" scandal of 1919 was found guilty.
4. False, "Casey at the Bat" was written by Ernest L. Thayer.
5. True
6. False, Bill Skowron's nickname "Moose" was short for Mussolini, a moniker his grandfather jokingly gave him as a child. Skowron, after being a standout Yankee first baseman for nine seasons, was traded to the Dodgers at the end of the 1962 season. The next year the Dodgers swept the Yankees in the World Series. Skowron went 5 for 13 with two doubles and a home run in the Series. Joe Pepitone, the player Skowron was traded for, hit only .154 without an extra base hit.
7. True, the Baltimore Orioles were a minor league team at the time.
8. True, Judge Kenesaw Mountain Landis was the first Commissioner. The position was created as a way to restore public confidence in baseball after the 1919 World Series scandal involving the Chicago White Sox. Landis was named by his father in honor of the site in Georgia where Landis' father, a Union Army surgeon during the Civil War, had been wounded. In 1915, Landis, as a federal judge, attempted to extradite Kaiser Wilhelm of Germany on a charge of murder after a German U-Boat torpedoed the luxury ocean liner *The Lusitania*, killing 1,100 passengers.
9. True
10. True
11. False, the team names were the New York Mets and the Houston Colt 45s.
12. True
13. False, Manny Mota holds the record with 150.
14. False; the American League record of 2,634 home runs was set in 1987. A total of 4,030 home runs were hit by both leagues in 1993, almost one third more than during the 1992 season.
15. False, Alexander Cartwright established the rules for that first organized baseball game in 1845.
16. True
17. True, exactly 70,257,938 people attended major league games in 1993. That figure represents actual ticket sales and doesn't allow for no-shows.

HEAD-TO-HEAD IN THE AL OUTFIELD

Can you answer these 18 questions about three standout outfielders and their 1993 seasons? The answers to questions 1-12 are found in the 1993 Box Score Comparison on the next page. Ten correct answers makes you a major-leaguer; 12 vaults you to all-star status.

a. Mike Greenwell   b. Kirby Puckett   c. Rickey Henderson
Red Sox   Twins   Athletics/Blue Jays

1. Who was the only one to hit over .300?

2. Who had the most at bats?

3. Who scored the most runs?

4. Who scored the fewest runs?

5. Who had the most hits?

6. Who had the fewest hits?

7. Who had the most extra base hits (not including home runs)?

8. Who had the fewest extra base hits?

9. Who hit the fewest home runs?

10. Who had the most RBI?

11. Who had the most stolen bases?

12. Who had the most errors?

EXTRA CREDIT

13. Whose first three major-league hits were home runs?

14. Who started in the All-Star Game, received the Gold Glove and the Silver Slugger Awards, and was his team's MVP in the same season?

15. Who was a Rookie of the Year?

a. Mike Greenwell
b. Kirby Puckett
c. Rickey Henderson
d. none of the above

16. Whose major league record did Rickey Henderson tie when he hit his 35th lead off home run?

a. Willie Mays
b. Steve Garvey
c. Bobby Bonds

17. Whose record did Rickey Henderson break when he set the record for the most stolen bases?

a. Lou Brock
b. Maury Wills
c. Ty Cobb

18. Which outfielder was the first major league player ever to have no home runs in one season and at least 30 a year later?

1993 Box Score Comparison

Player	AVG	AB	R	H	XBH	HR	RBI	S	E
a. Mike Greenwell	.316	534	76	169	44	13	72	5	2
b. Kirby Puckett	.293	615	87	180	42	21	88	8	2
c. Rickey Henderson	.288	476	112	137	24	21	59	53	7

Answers to questions 13-18:
13. a, Mike Greenwell, 14. b, Kirby Puckett; 15. d, none of the above; 16. c, Bobby Bonds; 17. a, Lou Brock; 18. b, Kirby Puckett

MAKING THE PITCH

Can you answer these multiple choice and true/false questions about pitching? Nine correct answers makes you a major-leaguer; 11 vaults you to all-star status.

1. Which of the following Atlanta Braves pitchers hasn't won a Cy Young Award?

a. Steve Avery
b. Greg Maddux
c. Tom Glavine

2. Which multiple Cy Young Award winner holds the record for the longest period of time between Cy Young wins (11 years)?

a. Carl Hubbell
b. Jim Palmer
c. Steve Carlton

3. Who set the major league record for games played without an error (319)?

a. Don Sutton
b. Gaylord Perry
c. Hoyt Wilhelm

4. Don Larsen pitched a perfect game in the 1956 World Series. One of the balls he used in that game came up for auction in October of 1993 in New York City. What did the ball sell for?

a. $725
b. $7,250
c. $17,250

5. Who holds the major league record for the most pitching appearances (987) without appearing in the World Series?

a. Lindy McDaniel
b. Gene Garber
c. Wilbur Wood

6. Who is the only pitcher to make appearances in more than one World Series and not retire a single batter?

a. Calvin Schiraldi
b. David West
c. Joe Sambito

7. True or false: Nolan Ryan never won a Cy Young Award.

8. True or false: Colorado first baseman Andres Galarraga had a .370 season batting average in 1993, but hit just .180 when the count contained two strikes.

9. True or false: Curt Schilling of Philadelphia, and Juan Guzman and Dave Stewart of Toronto weren't among the 25 highest paid pitchers in baseball in 1993.

10. True or false: The Atlanta Braves traded former Cy Young Award winner Mark Davis for minor league middle reliever Brad Hassinger during the 1993 season.

11. True or false: On April 23, 1993, Lee Smith passed Rollie Fingers as baseball's all-time save leader (358).

12. True or false: Yankee pitching prospect Brien Taylor received a $500,000 signing bonus despite starting the 1993 season at the minor league Double A level.

13. True or false: Lee Smith has never won the Cy Young Award.

14. True or false: In 1944, 17-year-old pitcher Joe Nuxhall became the youngest player to appear in a major league game. Starting for Cincinnati, he picked up the win in a 6-5 decision.

15. True or false: Joe Nuxhall was 6-5 with the Reds in 1944.

Answers: Making the Pitch

1. a, Steve Avery
2. c, Steve Carlton won the Cy Young Award in 1972 and again in 1982.
3. c, Hoyt Wilhelm
4. c; $17,250
5. a, Lindy McDaniel
6. b, David West ended the streak in the Game 4 of the 1993 World Series.
7. True
8. True
9. True
10. True, Mark Davis, the 1989 Cy Young Award winner as a member of the San Diego Padres, had one save while pitching for Atlanta and Kansas City in 1991 and 1992. He posted 44 saves and a 1.85 ERA the year he won the award. Davis returned to the Padres in 1993 after stints with the Royals, Braves and Phillies. He was 1-5 with a 4.12 ERA in 58 games.
11. False, Lee Smith did become the all-time save leader, but it was Jeff Reardon who had previously held the record, not Rollie Fingers.
12. False, Brien Taylor's signing bonus was $1.55 million, a record for an amateur. Taylor's mother, a cleaning lady, negotiated the deal.
13. True
14. False, Joe Nuxhall was 15 years old when he appeared in his first major league game. It made him the youngest player in league history. Nuxhall's performance proved he wasn't quite ready for the majors. Nuxhall, a Cincinnati native, signed with the Reds at the start of the 1944 season. Because he was still in high school, the Reds kept him on their major league roster rather than send him to the minors. Nuxhall would show up at Crosley Field and sit on the bench for night games and on weekends; and go to school during the week. Nuxhall made his major league debut on a sunny Saturday afternoon against the Cardinals, pitching two-thirds of an inning. The Reds were losing badly so Manager Bill McKechnie had Nuxhall pitch the ninth inning. Johnny Hopp, Marty Marion and Stan Musial were the Cardinals due to hit. Nuxhall walked Hopp and Marion before giving up a hit to Musial. By the time Nuxhall had finished, he had given up five earned runs, two hits and five walks. Nuxhall didn't return to the majors until 1952. He wound up having a decent major league career, winning 135 games and losing 117 with the Reds, Athletics and Angels. He was a better than average hitter for a pitcher, batting .198 lifetime with 15 home runs.
15. False

FORMERLY OWNED BY

Use the descriptions given to match the names of former major league owners. Six correct answers makes you a major-leaguer; seven vaults you to all-star status.

a. Harry Frazee   d. Walter O'Malley   g. Jake Ruppert

b. Ray Kroc   e. Clark Griffith   h. Tom Monaghan

c. Horace Stoneham   f. Charlie Finley   i. Charlie Comiskey

1. This controversial owner of the Kansas City Athletics, who later moved the team to Oakland, mixed show business, sales promotion and an ability to identify talented players. He was a very "hands on" owner, often publicly criticizing his players and firing managers at will. He once kicked a player off the team for making an error. His teams, however, won five straight division titles and three World Championships from 1971-1975. He suggested making every player a free agent at the conclusion of each season as a way of solving the dilemma of high salaries generated by free agency.

_____

2. This owner reportedly paid cash (about $48 million) for the Detroit Tigers during the 1980s with money earned from his Dominos pizza business. In 1993 he sold the Tigers to Mike Ilitch, the owner of Little Caesar's pizza.

_____

3. This owner and founder of McDonald's fast food restaurants, along with his wife, Joan, bought the San Diego Padres from C. Arnholt Smith in 1973. The purchase prevented Smith from moving the team to Washington, D.C. Smith was looking for a change after the Padres had lost more than 100 games during their first four seasons.

_____

4. This owner was a major league first baseman who became a major league manager and eventually a team owner. He purchased the Sioux City franchise that he later moved to St. Paul, Minnesota. In 1900 he moved the team again, this time to Chicago, where it became known as the White Stockings. His constant feuding with the players over salaries resulted in the infamous "Black Sox" scandal of 1919.

_____

5. This owner, a theatrical producer whose "hobby" was the Boston Red Sox, will never be forgiven by Sox fans for selling Babe Ruth to the rival New York Yankees for a mere $100,000 in December of 1919. He needed the money to produce the broadway show "No No Nanette." This owner is credited with introducing "The Star Spangled Banner" to the beginning of sporting events when he insisted the song be played before the start of the 1918 World Series.

_____

6. This owner became the most hated man in Brooklyn when he moved the Brooklyn Dodgers to Los Angeles in the late 1950s. He not only moved his team, but persuaded the owner of the New York Giants to move to San Francisco as well.

_____

7. This owner, nicknamed "The Old Fox," was a pitcher during the earliest days of professional baseball. He eventually became the sole owner of the Washington Senators. During his baseball career he won at least 20 games seven times. He was one of the first pitchers to "doctor" or scuff baseballs. The Washington Senators remained a family business and in 1961 his son, Calvin, moved the team to Minnesota and renamed it the Twins in honor of the twin cities of Minneapolis and St. Paul.

_____

8. This owner, better known as "The Colonel," was the owner of the New York Yankees during much of the first half of the 20th century. He was not afraid to open his checkbook and acquire players like Babe Ruth, Carl Mays, Joe Dugan and Sam Jones to make the Yankees the powerhouse team of the 1920s and 1930s. He paid approximately $450,000 for the Yankees in 1914 with family money from a New York brewery which he oversaw as its president.

_____

9. This owner, the former club president and owner of the New York Giants, moved the team to San Francisco after the 1957 season. In 1976 the team was almost sold to Labatt's Breweries in Toronto, but the sale was blocked by a court order. The club was then sold to Bob Lurie.

_____

Answers: Formerly Owned By

1. f, Charlie Finley
2. h, Tom Monaghan
3. b, Ray Kroc
4. i, Charlie Comiskey
5. a, Harry Frazee

6. d, Walter O'Malley
7. e, Clark Griffith
8. g, Jake Ruppert
9. c, Horace Stoneham

MORE FORMER OWNERS

Match the names of former major league baseball owners with their teams. Five correct answers makes you a major-leaguer; six vaults you to all-star status.

TEAMS	CHOICES
1. _____ Cleveland Indians	a. Bob Carpenter
2. _____ New York Mets	b. Roy Hofheinz
3. _____ Chicago Cubs	c. Charles Bronfman
4. _____ Seattle Mariners	d. Phillip Wrigley
5. _____ Pittsburgh Pirates	e. Bob Short
6. _____ Philadelphia Phillies	f. Joan Payson
7. _____ Houston Astros	g. Bing Crosby
8. _____ Montreal Expos	h. Bob Hope
9. _____ Texas Rangers	i. Lou Perini
10. _____ Atlanta Braves	j. George Argyros

Answers: More Former Owners

1. h, Bob Hope
2. f, Joan Payson
3. d, Phillip Wrigley
4. j, George Argyros
5. g, Bing Crosby

6. a, Bob Carpenter
7. b, Roy Hofheinz
8. c, Charles Bronfman
9. e, Bob Short
10. i, Lou Perini

CLASSIC YARDS

Can you answer these multiple choice questions about old big league ballparks? Six correct answers makes you a major-leaguer; eight vaults you to all-star status.

1. Where did the New York Giants play their home games?

a. Ebbets Field
b. Polo Grounds
c. Shibe Park

2. Where did the St. Louis Browns play their home games?

a. Griffith Stadium
b. Gaynor Park
c. Sportsman's Park

3. Where did the Seattle Pilots play their home games?

a. Sicks Stadium
b. Municipal Stadium
c. Fraiser Field

4. Who played their home games in County Stadium?

a. Milwaukee Braves
b. Kansas City Athletics
c. Washington Senators

5. Where is Colt Stadium located?

a. St. Louis
b. Houston
c. Kansas City

6. Where did the Brooklyn Dodgers play their home games?

a. Ebbets Field
b. Polo Grounds
c. Sportsman's Park

7. Where did the Philadelphia Athletics play their home games?

a. Huntington Avenue Ballpark
b. Arlington Stadium
c. Shibe Park

Answers: Classic Yards

1. b; Polo Grounds
2. c; Sportsman's Park
3. a; Sicks Stadium
4. a; Milwaukee Brewers

5. b; Houston
6. a; Ebbets Field
7. c; Shibe Park

WHO'S IN CHARGE?

Can you answer these multiple choice and true/false questions about managers? Eight correct answers makes you a major-leaguer; 10 vaults you to all-star status.

1. Who managed five consecutive World Champions?

a. John McGraw
b. Harry Wright
c. Casey Stengel

2. Who finished either first or second in his team's division 21 times in 29 seasons?

a. Sparky Anderson
b. John McGraw
c. Casey Stengel

3. What team did Casey Stengel manage before managing the New York Yankees and New York Mets?

a. Boston Bees
b. Brooklyn Dodgers
c. Chicago Cubs

4. Who was the first National League manager to win pennants in his first two seasons as manager?

a. Tommy Lasorda
b. Dallas Green
c. Bobby Cox

5. What pitching coach and long-time associate of manager Billy Martin supposedly was an expert at teaching major league pitchers to throw the spitball?

a. Rick Wise
b. Art Fowler
c. Stan Williams

6. In 1977, Frank Robinson became the first black manager in major league history when he was named manager of what team?

a. Atlanta Braves
b. Baltimore Orioles
c. Cleveland Indians

7. Who was the first manager to win a pennant in the National and American Leagues?

a. Joe McCarthy
b. Gene Mauch
c. Yogi Berra

8. Who is the only manager to win a World Series in the National and American Leagues?

a. Casey Stengel
b. Yogi Berra
c. Sparky Anderson

9. Who was given a one-year suspension in 1947 by the Commissioner of Baseball for associating with known gamblers?

a. Billy Southworth
b. Leo Durocher
c. Bucky Harris

10. How many managers did George Steinbrenner place at the helm of the New York Yankees during his first 20 years as team owner (1973-93)?

a. 15
b. 20
c. 25
d. 30

11. What is Detroit Tiger Manager Sparky Anderson's nickname?

a. Captain Hook
b. Captain Midnight
c. Captain Bligh

12. Who is the second-winningest major league manager behind Philadelphia Athletics manager/owner Connie Mack?

a. Bucky Harris
b. Walter Alston
c. John McGraw
d. Gene Mauch

13. True or false: 1993 New York Met Manager Dallas Green is the second Mets manager to have managed both the Mets and the Yankees.

14. True or false: Gene Mauch, who managed in the major leagues for 35 years, managed a team that went to the World Series only once.

15. True or false: In 1993, Cubs Manager Jim Lefebvre was fired after leading the Cubs to only their third winning season since 1972. Lefebvre was the 10th Cub manager in as many years.

16. True or false: In 1993, Tiger Manager Sparky Anderson became only the third manager in major league history to reach 2,000 victories.

17. True or false: Stan Wasiak was known as the "King of the Minors." He set minor league records with 37 consecutive seasons as a manager, winning 2,570 games between 1950 and 1986.

Answers: Who's in Charge?

1. c, Casey Stengel managed the Yankees to World Championships from 1949 to 1953.

   Billy Martin was never afraid to speak his mind about owners, players or even other managers. With the exception of Casey Stengel, Martin said Charlie Dressen was the best and smartest manager he ever played for.

   Dressen managed the 1952 and 1953 pennant-winning Brooklyn Dodgers. Despite his success, Dressen was fired by Owner Walter O'Malley because of Dressen's insistence on a two-year contract. O'Malley objected because policy was, and still is, to only sign Dodger managers to one-year contracts. O'Malley replaced Dressen with Walter Alston, who very much later was replaced by Tommy Lasorda. Alston and Lasorda have combined to manage the Dodgers for more than 40 years, coming to terms with a new contract every 12 months.

   Martin believed former Yankee Dick Howser was an outstanding manager; he respected fellow manager Dick Williams for his aggressiveness; and once described Atlanta Braves Manager Bobby Cox as "brilliant." Martin thought Sparky Anderson was overrated and Gene Mauch over-managed, sometimes outsmarting himself by utilizing too much personnel from his bench while playing for a single run too early in the game.

   When Stengel was managing the Mets he instituted a midnight curfew. The penalty for being caught out after hours was a stiff fine. Once during a road trip a handful of players came into the hotel after midnight. When they got on the elevator to go to their rooms the operator asked them to autograph a baseball. At the pregame meeting the next day, Stengel appeared with the ball and ordered the violators into his office. It turns out the elevator operator was working with Stengel to catch players breaking curfew.

2. c, John "Little Napoleon" McGraw managed the New York Giants to 10 pennants and three World Championships.

3. b, Casey Stengel launched his managing career with the Dodgers (1934-36) and later moved to Boston (1938-43). From there he managed in the minor leagues until 1949, when he was chosen to manage the Yankees. He finished his career with the expansion New York Mets in 1965.

4. a, Tommy Lasorda won the National League pennant his first two years as manager for the Los Angeles Dodgers (1977-78), but lost in six games to the Yankees both times.

5. b, In 1970, Art Fowler, still pitching at age 49, won nine games and saved 15 more with Denver in the American Association. It's said he was voted league MVP that year but refused the award because it didn't mean very much to him at his age. He thought it would be best to give the award to a young player.

6. c, Frank Robinson was the only player in history to be voted the MVP in the National and American League; first with the Reds in 1961 and again with the Orioles in 1966. He led Baltimore to a pennant and the World Championship that year. Robinson not only excelled on the field, but in the clubhouse as well. It usually was in the form of encouragement or a joke. One humorous story involved Robinson, Moe Drabowsky and Paul Blair, and focused on Blair's fear of snakes. Each day Robinson carried a briefcase to work. One day Robinson pulled a rubber snake from the briefcase and tossed it at the terrified Blair. For days, Robinson and others continued to startle Blair with fake reptiles. The joke climaxed a few days later when Drabowsky entered the clubhouse with a live boa constrictor. Blair,

thinking it was just another rubber snake, didn't react when approached with the creature – that is, until the boa constrictor flicked his tongue in his direction. Those who witnessed the prank said Blair's feet barely touched the ground as he fled the locker room. Blair refused to return to the locker room and dressed for the day's game in the dugout. In 1975 Robinson became the player/manager of the Cleveland Indians, probably the last major leaguer to have both responsibilities simultaneously. Player/managers were common in the big leagues through the 1930s. Robinson went on to manage the Giants and Orioles, and in 1993 was still with the Orioles in their front office as a vice president. Robinson gave up managing in 1989. In September of that season, he and Toronto Manager Cito Gaston made major league history as the first black managers to appear in the same game.

7. a, Joe McCarthy
8. c, Sparky Anderson
9. b, Leo Durocher
10. b, 20
11. a, Captain Hook
12. c, John McGraw managed teams that won 2,840 games. Connie Mack had the luxury of never being worried about being fired because he owned the team in addition to managing it. There were many seasons he would have probably been fired if he had worked for someone other than himself.
13. False, Yogi Berra and Casey Stengel managed the Yankees and Mets.
14. False, Gene Mauch never managed a team that made it to the World Series.
15. True
16. False, Sparky Anderson was the seventh manager to win 2,000 games.
17. True

HEAD-TO-HEAD AT SECOND BASE

Can you answer these 20 questions about three standout second basemen and their 1993 seasons? The answers to questions 1-16 are found in the 1993 Box Score Comparison on the next page. Nine correct answers makes you a major-leaguer; 11 vaults you to all-star status.

a. Jeff Kent
   New York Mets

b. Scott Fletcher
   Boston Red Sox

c. Ryne Sandberg
   Chicago Cubs

1. Who hit better than .300 in 1993?

2. Who had the lowest batting average?

3. Who had the most at bats?

4. Who had the fewest at bats?

5. Who scored the most runs?

6. Who scored the fewest runs?

7. All three were within 12 hits of each other. Within which range did they fall?

a. 130-142
b. 143-155
c. 157-169

8. Who had the highest number of extra base hits, not including home runs?

9. Who had the fewest extra base hits?

10. Who hit the most home runs?

11. Who had the fewest home runs?

12. Who had the most RBI?

13. Who had the most stolen bases?

14. Who stole the fewest bases?

15. Who made the most errors?

16. Who made the fewest errors?

EXTRA CREDIT

17. Who annually earns roughly twice as much money as the other two combined?

18. Who was involved in a trade for pitcher David Cone?

19. Who started his major league career in Philadelphia?

20. Who started his major league career with the Chicago Cubs?

1993 Box Score Comparison

Player	AVG	AB	R	H	XBH	HR	RBI	S	E
a. Jeff Kent	.268	488	63	131	24	20	78	4	22
b. Scott Fletcher	.286	479	81	137	38	5	45	16	11
c. Ryne Sandberg	.309	456	67	141	20	9	45	9	7

Answers to questions 17-20:

17. c, Ryne Sandberg; 18. a, Jeff Kent; 19. c, Ryne Sandberg; 20. b, Scott Fletcher

1993 GOLD GLOVERS

Using the list of names provided, fill in the blanks with 1993 the Gold Glove winners. An added challenge is the fact that some of the teams are not provided. Good luck!

AMERICAN LEAGUE

a. Robin Ventura

e. Lou Whitaker

h. Don Mattingly

b. Omar Vizquel

f. Kenny Lofton

i. Devon White

c. Mark Langston

g. Roberto Alomar

j. Tom Henke

d. Joe Carter

Team	Position	Player
1. California	Pitcher	_____
2. _____	Catcher	Ivan Rodriquez
3. _____	First base	_____
4. _____	Second base	_____
5. Chicago	Third base	_____
6. _____	Shortstop	_____
7. Cleveland	Outfield	_____
8. _____	Outfield	Ken Griffey, Jr.
9. Toronto	Outfield	_____

NATIONAL LEAGUE

a. Robby Thompson   e. Jeff Kent   h. John Smoltz

b. Phil Plantier   f. Larry Walker   i. Kurt Manwaring

c. Greg Maddux   g. Matt Williams   j. Lenny Dykstra

d. Jay Bell

Team	Position	Name
1. Atlanta	Pitcher	_____
2. _____	Catcher	_____
3. _____	First base	Mark Grace
4. _____	Second base	_____
5. San Francisco	Third base	_____
6. _____	Shortstop	_____
7. Montreal Expos	Outfield	_____
8. _____	Outfield	Marquis Grissom
9. _____	Outfield	_____

Answers: 1993 Gold Glovers

AMERICAN LEAGUE

Team	Position	Name
1. California	Pitcher	Mark Langston
2. Texas	Catcher	Ivan Rodriquez
3. New York	First base	Don Mattingly
4. Toronto	Second base	Roberto Alomar
5. Chicago	Third base	Robin Ventura
6. Seattle	Shortstop	Omar Vizquel
7. Cleveland	Outfield	Kenny Lofton
8. Seattle	Outfield	Ken Griffey, Jr.
9. Toronto	Outfield	Devon White

NATIONAL LEAGUE

Team	Position	Name
1. Atlanta	Pitcher	Greg Maddux
2. San Francisco	Catcher	Kurt Manwaring
3. Chicago	First base	Mark Grace
4. San Francisco	Second base	Robby Thompson
5. San Francisco	Third base	Matt Williams
6. Pittsburgh	Shortstop	Jay Bell
7. Montreal	Outfield	Larry Walker
8. Montreal	Outfield	Marquis Grissom
9. San Francisco	Outfield	Barry Bonds

BREAKING THE COLOR BARRIER

During the first half of the 20th century there were scores of tremendously talented baseball players who, because of the color of their skin, weren't allowed to play in the major or minor leagues. Their exclusion was racism at its worst. The "whites only" policy reflected both the attitudes of baseball owners (all the way down the line to the bat boys) and the majority of the white American society as well.

In 1946, Branch Rickey, the General Manager of the Brooklyn Dodgers, broke the color barrier by signing Jackie Robinson to a minor league contract. Rickey was the first major league administrator to accept the fact that players from the Negro Leagues could make an impact on major league baseball. He knew blacks could be the difference between winning and losing as well as increasing gate receipts.

Robinson's first assignment was in Montreal where he became the first black player in the International League. Robinson led the league in hitting as well as in runs scored his first year as the Montreal Royals finished in first place with an impressive 19 1/2-game lead.

Robinson would have probably been just as successful had he skipped the minors and joined the Dodgers, but Rickey wisely decided to gauge the public's acceptance of Robinson in Canada before moving him to the majors.

The next year Robinson was with the Dodgers and they preceded to win seven National League pennants between 1947 and 1956. Robinson was voted the National League's Rookie of the Year in 1947 and was league MVP two years later.

Robinson definitely showed the nation that the color of a man's skin had nothing to do with the ability to play baseball. Despite the successes of Robinson and other black players like Don Newcome and Roy Campanella, other teams resisted signing blacks. It wasn't until 1959 that every major league team had at least one black player on its roster.

Many of the early blacks to reach the major leagues were poor choices. Some speculate they were hand-picked to fail so teams could claim a black player on the roster, but justify not playing him.

Robinson certainly wasn't that type of player. He was a marvelous athlete, a college graduate and an officer in the United States Army during World War II. Most of all, Robinson had the strength of character to endure and overcome the bigotry he faced almost every day early in his major league career.

Robinson was a standout student-athlete at UCLA, and the school's first to letter in four sports. In addition to baseball, Robinson led the Pacific Coast Conference in scoring twice as a basketball player; led the nation with a better than 11-yard per carry average in football as a running back one season; and set a conference record in the broad jump as a member of the Bruin track and field team.

After graduation, Robinson played professional football with the Los Angeles Bulldogs until the start of World War II when he joined the Army. Immediately after enlisting, Robinson was sent to Officer Candidate School in Kansas and graduated as a second lieutenant. In 1944, Robinson was threatened with a court martial after an incident involving a bus driver ordering him to sit in the back of an army bus. Robinson was never formally charged but rather than endure a military court hearing, Robinson resigned his commission and was honorably discharged.

Jackie Robinson broke major league baseball's color barrier when he joined the Brooklyn Dodgers in 1947.

Can you determine which team these famous black major leaguers played for? Each individual was the first African-American to play for his team. Six correct answers makes you a major-leaguer; eight vaults you to all-star status.

AMERICAN LEAGUE

a. Boston Red Sox

b. Chicago White Sox

c. Cleveland Indians

d. New York Yankees

e. Detroit Tigers

f. Philadelphia Athletics

g. St. Louis Browns

h. Washington Senators

1. Lary Doby: When team owner Bill Veeck signed Doby in 1947 he became the first African-American to play in the American League. Doby was always grateful to Veeck for the opportunity and considered him a spiritual godfather. In his first full season (1948), Doby hit .301 with 16 HRs and his team won the World Championship. During Game 4 of that World Series, Doby hit the game-winning home run off the Braves' Johnny Sain. Lifetime Doby hit .283 with 253 HRs.

_____

2. Hank Thompson: Thompson was the second African-American to play in the American League (1947). He later moved to a National League team and also was its first black player. Thompson became the first black hitter to face a black pitcher when he went up against Don Newcome in the 1949 World Series. During his career Thompson played 933 games at second base and hit .267 with 129 HRs and 482 RBI.

_____

3. Sam Hairston: This catcher's major league career consisted of two games. It is a mystery why this team chose to sign, as its first black player, someone who wasn't considered to have the skills to play in the major leagues. Hairston did, however, become a baseball scout and the father of two sons who played in the majors: Jerry, who had a 13-year career with the Pittsburgh Pirates; and John, a Chicago Cub in 1969.

_____

4. Bob Trice: Trice, a pitcher, was signed in 1953 and played through the 1955 season. Lifetime, his record was 9-9 with a 5.80 ERA.

_____

5. Carlos Paula: Paula was signed in 1954 and spent the season on the bench. In nine games he hit .167. He was given a chance to play regularly in 1955, seeing action in 115 games. Paula responded with a .299 batting average, six HRs and 45 RBI. His last season was 1956, when he hit just .183 in 33 games.

_____

6. Elston Howard: Howard, a catcher, came to the majors in 1955 at age 26. The American League team that signed him already had a standout catcher, so Elston played mostly outfield during the first five years of his career. Given an opportunity behind the plate, Howard proved himself an excellent defensive catcher with a .993 career fielding average. He also was a force at the plate, hitting over .300 three times; including .348 in 1961. His lifetime average was

.274 with 167 HRs. Howard played on the Amercian League All-Star team nine consecutive times and in 1963 was the league's MVP. After his playing career ended, Howard coached in the majors for 11 years. Howard is credited with inventing the heavy donut that on-deck hitters slip over their bats when warming up to hit. Howard and Pee Wee Reese share the major league record for playing on the most World Series losing teams.

_____

7. Ozzie Virgil: Virgil, a third baseman, was the first Dominican native to play in the major leagues. He played every position except pitcher during his career. Virgil went on to coach four different teams after retiring as a player. From 1956 to 1969 he played in 324 games and hit .231 with 14 HRs and 73 RBI.

_____

8. Pumpsie Green: Green joined the last major league team to integrate its roster. During Green's four-year career, playing second base, he hit .246 with 13 HRs and 74 RBI.

_____

NATIONAL LEAGUE

a. Boston Braves

b. Brooklyn Dodgers

c. Chicago Cubs

d. Cincinnati Reds

e. New York Giants

f. Philadelphia Phillies

g. Pittsburgh Pirates

h. St. Louis Cardinals

1. Jackie Robinson: Robinson was the first African-American to play in the major leagues, and was 28 years old at the time. Lary Doby started playing in the American League later during that 1947 season.

_____

2. Hank Thompson: Thompson signed with a National League team for the 1949 season. During the 1947 season he played in the American League, and therefore has the distinction of being the first black player to play in both leagues.

_____

3. Sam Jethro: Jethro was a switch-hitting outfielder who became the National League Rookie of the Year in his first season (1950). He claimed to be only 28 years old at the time but was likely much older because of his rapid decline. He played in 442 games, hitting .261 with 49 HRs. Jethro was an excellent base-stealer and led the league in steals his first two seasons with 35 each year.

_____

4. Ernie Banks: Banks joined this National League team in 1953 and is still there today. He played more than 2,500 games at shortstop, hit 512 HRs and was elected to the Hall of Fame in 1977.

———————————

5. Tom Alston: From 1954 to 1957, Alston mostly sat on the bench. The first baseman's best year was his first, hitting .244 in 66 games.

———————————

6. Curt Roberts: During Roberts' three-year major league career he played in 171 games as a backup infielder. He was a good fielder and hit .223.

———————————

7. Nino Escalera: Escalera was signed in 1954 as an outfielder but was used mostly as a pinch-hitter. In his lone major-league season, Escalera appeared in 73 games and hit .159 with three RBI.

———————————

8. John Irvin Kennedy: In 1957 Kennedy played in five games, had two at-bats and played third base.

———————————

Answers: *Breaking the Color Barrier*

AMERICAN LEAGUE

1. c, Cleveland Indians
2. g, St. Louis Browns
3. b, Chicago White Sox
4. f, Philadelphia Athletics
5. h, Washington Senators
6. d, New York Yankees
7. e, Detroit Tigers
8. a, Boston Red Sox

NATIONAL LEAGUE

1. b, Brooklyn Dodgers
2. e, New York Giants
3. a, Boston Braves
4. c, Chicago Cubs
5. h, St. Louis Cardinals
6. g, Pittsburgh Pirates
7. d, Cincinnati Reds
8. f, Philadelphia Phillies

1970s & 1980s

Can you answer these multiple choice questions about baseball in the 1970s and 1980s? Twelve correct answers makes you a major-leaguer; 15 vaults you to all-star status.

1. Two members of the 1976 Cincinnati Reds were the most recent teammates to finish first and second in RBI. Joe Morgan was runner-up that year. Who finished first?

a. Johnny Bench
b. George Foster
c. Ken Griffey

2. Shortstop Tony Fernandez broke the record for total RBI in a World Series when he drove in his eighth and ninth runs during Game 4 of the 1993 Series. Who held the previous record?

a. Rick Burleson
b. Bucky Dent
c. Al Weiss

3. In 1979 who became the first designated hitter to be selected American League MVP?

a. George Bell
b. Jeff Burroughs
c. Don Baylor

4. Two of the following players entered the major leagues having never played in the minors. Who played in the minors?

a. Al Kaline
b. Jim "Catfish" Hunter
c. Joe Pepitone

5. Who led the National League with 1,533 hits during the 1980s?

a. Dale Murphy
b. Keith Hernandez
c. Andre Dawson

6. What pair of brothers won the Cy Young Award in the 1970s?

a. Joe and Phil Niekro
b. Jim and Gaylord Perry
c. Paul and Rick Reuschel

7. There are three post-World War II players with over 10,000 at bats but less than 3,000 hits. All three are listed below. Who doesn't belong?

a. Brooks Robinson
b. Mark Belanger
c. Frank Robinson
d. Luis Aparicio

8. What foreign-born player leads all foreign-born players with 3,053 career hits?

a. Rod Carew
b. Tony Perez
c. Luis Aparicio

9. Who was named Minor League Player of the Year twice during the 1980s?

a. Jose Canseco
b. Gregg Jefferies
c. Dwight Gooden

10. In 1980 who set the major league record of 184 singles in a season?

a. Tony Gwynn
b. Wade Boggs
c. Willie Wilson

11. Which National Leaguer led the majors with 2,045 hits during the 1970s?

a. Lou Brock
b. Pete Rose
c. Larry Bowa

12. Who led the American League with 1,787 hits in the 1970s?

a. Bobby Murcer
b. Amos Otis
c. Rod Carew

13. What San Francisco Giant established a baseball first when he gave up three back-to-back home runs in the first inning of a game against San Diego on April 13, 1987?

a. Jim Gott
b. Roger Mason
c. Dave Dravecky

14. Who hit into the fewest double plays, 33 in over 4,500 at bats, while with the Orioles in the 1970s?

a. Don Buford
b. Paul Blair
c. Al Bumbry

15. What shortstop retired in the 1980s with the National League record for games played at that position (2,222)?

a. Larry Bowa
b. Bud Harrelson
c. Bill Russell

16. The National League was 19-1 in All-Star Games played between 1962 and 1983. The American League's lone win was in 1971. What pitcher got the win?

a. Blue Moon Odom
b. Ken Holtzman
c. Vida Blue

17. Who was the last player in the American League to have more than 200 hits with less than 40 extra base hits?

a. Cesar Tovar
b. Rod Carew
c. Dan Gladden

18. Who was the last player in the National League to have more than 200 hits with less than 40 extra base hits?

a. Tony Gwynn
b. Brett Butler
c. Steve Sax

19. Who, in the 1980s, played his last three seasons with three different teams, yet made it to the World Series each year?

a. Paul Blair
b. Don Baylor
c. Al Bumbry

20. Nolan Ryan broke the all-time strikeout record on April 17, 1983. Whose record did he break?

a. Lefty Grove
b. Cy Young
c. Walter Johnson

EXTRA CREDIT
1. True or false: Chicago Cub Ernie Banks set the career record for the best fielding percentage by a shortstop.

2. True or false: The famous fashion designer Geoffrey Beame designed a line of clothing which included Steve Garvey's name during the 1970s.

3. True or false: Jim Nettles (brother of Graig Nettles) had the lowest batting average among players with at least 1,500 at bats during the 1970s.

4. True or false: Reliever Jeff Reardon had 30 or more saves in five consecutive seasons during the 1980s.

Answers: 1970s & 1980s

1. b, George Foster. He hit .429 (6 for 14) with four RBI against New York in the World Series that year. The catchers for both teams stole the spotlight, however. Cincinnati's Johnny Bench hit .533 (8 for 15) with two HRs, a triple, a double, six RBI and four runs scored. The Yankees' Thurman Munson hit .529 (9 for 17) and had two RBI. New York scored just eight runs and lost the Series 4-0.
2. b, Bucky Dent batted .417, scored three runs and had a record seven RBI in the 1978 World Series between the Dodgers and Yankees.
3. c, Don Baylor
4. c, Joe Pepitone almost didn't have a career in baseball, or anywhere thanks to a 38-caliber bullet. He grew up in a tough Brooklyn (N.Y.) neighborhood and was shot in the stomach one day while at school in 1958. A priest was called to administer the last rites to Pepitone. He survived and the

Yankees signed him to a minor league contract later that same year. Pepitone made the major league roster in 1962 and was the starting first baseman a year later. He retired in 1973. In 1985, Pepitone was stopped by Brooklyn police for running a stop light. Inside his car, the police found cocaine, heroin, pills, drug paraphernalia and a loaded pistol. Pepitone spent six months in prison before being released into a work release program within the Yankees' front office.

5. a, Dale Murphy
6. b, Jim and Gaylord Perry
7. b, Mark Belanger. Brooks Robinson, Frank Robinson, Luis Aparicio and Rabbit Maranville are the only major leaguers with less than 3,000 hits in at least 10,000 at bats. Everyone except Maranville played during the post World War II era. Maranville played from 1912 to 1935.
8. a, Panama native Rod Carew had 3,053 career

hits, ahead of Tony Perez (Cuba, 2,732) and Luis Aparicio (Venezuela, 2,667).

9. b, Gregg Jefferies was the Minor League Player of the Year in 1986 and 1987.

10. c, Willie Wilson

11. b, Pete Rose. No one else had more than 1,800.

12. c, Rod Carew

13. b, Roger Mason. The Giants came back to win that game as Jim Gott got the win and Dave Dravecky the loss. Ironically, Mason was a standout for Philadelphia during the 1993 World Series.

14. a, Don Buford

15. a, Larry Bowa

16. c, Vida Blue

17. b, Rod Carew, 38 extra base hits among 218 hits.

18. a, Tony Gwynn, 36 extra base hits among 213 hits.

19. b, Don Baylor

20. c, Walter Johnson

Extra Credit Answers:

1. False, Larry Bowa

2. False, Reggie Jackson

3. False, Jim Mason

4. True

HEAD-TO-HEAD AT THIRD BASE

Can you answer these 19 questions about three standout third basemen and their 1993 seasons? The answers to questions 1-15 are found in the 1993 Box Score Comparison on the next page. Nine correct answers makes you a major-leaguer; 11 vaults you to all-star status.

a. Wade Boggs
   New York Yankees

b. Terry Pendleton
   Atlanta Braves

c. Charlie Hayes
   Colorado Rockies

1. Who had a batting average above .300?

2. Who had the lowest batting average?

3. Who had more than 600 at bats?

4. The trio's runs scored totals were within 12 of each other. Within what range do they fall?

a. 61-75
b. 76-90
c. 91-105

5. The trio's hit totals were also close to each other. Within what range do they fall?

a. 150-165
b. 166-175
c. 176-190

6. Who had the most extra base hits?

7. Who had the most home runs?

8. Who hit only two home runs?

9. Who had the most RBI?

10. Who had the fewest RBI?

11. Who had the most stolen bases?

12. Who didn't steal a single base?

13. Who made the most errors?

14. Who made the fewest errors?

15. Who had the fewest extra base hits?

EXTRA CREDIT

16. Who used to play for the St. Louis Cardinals?

17. Who used to play for the Boston Red Sox?

18. Who used to play for the New York Yankees?

19. Who used to play for the Philadelphia Phillies?

1993 Box Score Comparison

Player	AVG	AB	R	H	XBH	HR	RBI	S	E
a. Wade Boggs	.300	556	83	166	27	2	59	0	12
b. Terry Pendleton	.269	625	79	168	33	17	80	5	19
c. Charlie Hayes	.305	573	89	175	47	25	98	11	20

Answers to questions 16-19:
16. b, Terry Pendleton; 17. a, Wade Boggs; 18. c, Charlie Hayes; 19. c, Charlie Hayes

BEST OF THE BEST

Can you answer these multiple choice and true/false questions about Cy Young, Gold Glove and MVP Award winners? Thirteen correct answers makes you a major-leaguer; 16 vaults you to all-star status.

CY YOUNG AWARD

1. Who won the 1993 American League Cy Young Award?

a. Juan Guzman
b. Jack McDowell
c. Randy Johnson

2. Who won the first American League Cy Young Award in 1958?

a. Dean Chance
b. Bob Turley
c. Whitey Ford

3. Two pitchers tied for the American League Cy Young Award in 1969. One was Baltimore's Mike Cueller. With whom did Cueller share the award?

a. Jim Lonborg
b. Jim Palmer
c. Denny McLain

4. Who is the most recent American Leaguer to win the Cy Young Award in two consecutive seasons?

a. Roger Clemens
b. Bret Saberhagen
c. Bob Welch

5. What American League reliever is the most recent Cy Young Award winner?

a. Bobby Thigpen
b. Jeff Reardon
c. Dennis Eckersley

6. No American Leaguer has won four Cy Young Awards, but three have won it three times. Which of the following Cy Young Award winners isn't a three-time winner.

a. Roger Clemens
b. Jim Palmer
c. Denny McLain
d. Whitey Ford

GOLD GLOVE AWARD

1. Who has won the most Gold Glove Awards at first base?

a. Keith Hernandez
b. Don Mattingly
c. George Scott

2. Which catcher has won the most Gold Gloves?

a. Johnny Bench
b. Carlton Fisk
c. Bob Boone

3. Which pitcher has won the most Gold Gloves?

a. Steve Carlton
b. Jim Kaat
c. Bob Gibson

4. Who has won the most Gold Gloves overall?

a. Ozzie Smith
b. Willie Mays
c. Brooks Robinson

5. True or false: New York Yankee first baseman Don Mattingly has won the American League Gold Glove at first base eight of the last nine years. Detroit's Cecil Fielder interrupted Mattingly's streak in 1990.

6. True or false: Gold Glove Awards were first presented in 1977.

7. True or false: The only designated hitter to win a Gold Glove was Don Baylor in 1979.

MVPs

1. True or false: Babe Ruth was named the American League MVP only once.

2. True or false: New York Yankee first baseman Lou Gehrig was never the American League MVP.

3. True or false: Yankee teammates Yogi Berra and Mickey Mantle were each named MVP three times.

4. True or false: Yankee Joe DiMaggio and his brother, Boston center fielder Dom DiMaggio, were named MVP at least once.

5. True or false: Yankees Yogi Berra, Mickey Mantle and Roger Maris were named MVP in consecutive seasons.

6. True or false: Yankee shortstop and eventual New York broadcaster Phil Rizzuto was never named MVP.

7. True or false: The first designated hitter to be named a MVP was Yankee Ron Blomberg.

8. True or false: Roger Maris was the American League MVP in 1960 and 1961. Both times Maris' teammate Mickey Mantle was runner-up. Only seven combined votes separated the two among the voters.

9. True or false: Ted Williams and Joe DiMaggio, two dominating players during the 1940s, were each two-time MVP Award winners.

Answers: Best of the Best

CY YOUNG AWARD

1. b, Jack McDowell
2. b, Bob Turley
3. c, Denny McLain
4. a, Roger Clemens
5. c, Dennis Eckersley
6. d, Whitey Ford won once (1961)

GOLD GLOVE AWARD

1. a, Keith Hernandez
2. a, Johnny Bench
3. b, Jim Kaat
4. c, Third baseman Brooks Robinson
5. False, Mark McGuire won the award in 1990. Cecil Fielder has never won a Gold Glove.
6. False, The award began in 1957.
7. False, Designated hitters don't receive the award.

MVPs

1. True
2. False, Lou Gehrig was MVP twice.
3. True
4. False, Dom DiMaggio was never an MVP.
5. True
6. False, Phil Rizzuto was the MVP in 1950.
7. False, Don Baylor was the first designated hitter to be MVP.
8. True, The voting in 1960 was 225-222 and the voting in 1961 was 202-198.
9. False, Joe DiMaggio was a three-time winner.

1950s & 1960s

Can you answer these multiple choice questions about baseball in the 1950s and 1960s? Seven correct answers makes you a major-leaguer; nine vaults you to all-star status.

1. Who was the only player during the 1950s to be named the National League MVP three times?

a. Ernie Banks
b. Willie Mays
c. Roy Campanella

2. Who hit the first grand slam home run in a World Series?

a. Willie Mays
b. Chuck Hiller
c. Jim Davenport

3. In 1960, Philadelphia Phillies Manager Eddie Sawyer quit after the first game of the season. Who replaced him as manager of the team that came to be known as the "Whiz Kids?"

a. Dick Williams
b. Gene Mauch
c. Eddie Stankey

4. What Philadelphia Phillies outfielder led the league in putouts a major league record nine times?

a. Richie Ashburn
b. Dick Sisler
c. Del Ennis

5. Billy Martin's career was checkered by reports of fist fights. With whom did he have his first documented fight with when he reached the major leagues?

a. Matt Batts
b. Clint Courtney
c. Jimmy Piersall
d. Phil Rizzuto

6. Who holds the distinction of being the losing pitcher when Early Wynn won his 300th game and throwing the pitch that allowed Stan Musial to record his 3,000th hit?

a. Moe Drabowsky
b. Bob Miller
c. Vinegar Bend Mizell

7. Which New York Yankee holds the record for the longest World Series hitting streak (17 games)?

a. Gil McDougald
b. Gene Woodling
c. Hank Bauer

8. Who holds the record for leading the majors in games won by a pitcher eight times?

a. Warren Spahn
b. Bob Lemon
c. Bob Turley

9. Who holds the record for striking out the most times in a single season?

a. Ken Griffey
b. Bobby Bonds
c. Hal McRae
d. Felipe Alou

10. What position did Mickey Mantle play during his first season with the New York Yankees?

a. Outfield
b. First base
c. Shortstop

11. The 1993 Atlanta Braves had two 20-game winners for the first time since 1959. Warren Spahn was one of the 20-game winners in 1959. Who was the other?

a. Don McMahon
b. Lou Burdette
c. Johnny Sain

12. Boston's Carl Yastrzemski and Rico Petrocelli made World Series history in 1967 when they teamed with one other person to each hit a home run in the same half-inning. Who was the third Red Sox player to go deep that inning?

a. Elston Howard
b. George Scott
c. Reggie Smith

Answers: 1950s & 1960s

1. c, Roy Campanella
2. b, San Francisco's Chuck Hiller did it in 1962 against the Yankees. He hit .269 with three doubles, five RBI and a homer in that Series. Willie Mays hit only .250 and Jim Davenport only .136 as the Yankees won the Series 4-3.
3. b, Gene Mauch.

   Eddie Stanky, after managing the Cardinals and White Sox during parts of the 1950s and 1960s, returned during the 1977 season to manage the Texas Rangers, but quit after one game. Stanky said the game and the players had changed and he wasn't going to change with them. When Stanky managed the White Sox, he placed game balls in a freezer. He believed the reduced temperatures deadened the balls and they did not travel as far. Conversely, managers with teams possessing a lot of power would heat baseballs in an oven, thinking the ball would carry farther when it left the bat.

4. a, Richie Ashburn
5. c, Billy Martin's first recorded fight was with Red Sox rookie shortstop Jimmy Piersall. He tangled with Browns' catcher Clint "Scrap Iron" Courtney in June of that season, too. There was a rematch the following April when Martin took exception to a collision at second base between Courtney and Phil Rizzuto during a game played in St. Louis. Martin's third major-league bout, and fourth overall, was with Detroit catcher Matt Batts a few months later.

Piersall's story is unique because the pressures of playing major league baseball contributed to him eventually being admitted to a mental institution. He joined the Red Sox as a center fielder but was moved to shortstop. Piersall, who regularly experienced chronic headaches, couldn't cope with playing a new position as a major-league rookie. His behavior both on the field and off became so erratic that Red Sox management convinced him to check into a private sanitarium. While there, Piersall became violent and was soon transferred to the Danvers (Mass.) State Hospital for electroconvulsive shock treatment. Piersall's illness climaxed when he woke up one morning in August of 1952 with no memory of the previous eight months. He had no recollection of attending spring training or playing in 50 regular-season games with the Red Sox. Even the memories of his wife and family were gone. He was moved to the Westborough State Hospital, where he eventually fully recovered. Overall, Piersall was institutionalized for six weeks. He returned to baseball, and played center field for 17 years and hit .272. *Fear Strikes Out*, a book and movie, vividly tells the story of Piersall's life and traumas.

6. a; relief pitcher Moe Drabowsky
7. c; Hank Bauer. His record was almost broken in 1993 when Toronto catcher Pat Borders' post-season hitting streak ended at 16 games. When Borders was asked about Bauer, he said, "I've heard of him, but I don't really know who he is."
8. a; Warren Spahn, the winningest left-handed pitcher in major league history, holds the major league record for leading the league in total wins (eight times).
9. b; Bobby Bonds, in 1969, set a major league record when he struck out 185 times. In 1970, he struck out 189 times.
10. c; shortstop. Mickey Mantle was the triple crown winner in 1956, hitting .353 with 52 HRs and 130 RBI. At the end of the season he received a modest raise. The next year Mantle hit .365 with 34 HRs and 94 RBI. During contract negotiations between Mantle and General Manager George Weiss, management wanted Mantle to take a pay cut, noting Mantle's season statistics were down from 1956. Mantle refused, and the two sides agreed to pay him his 1957 salary.
11. b; Lou Burdette
12. c; Reggie Smith

HEAD-TO-HEAD AT SHORTSTOP

Can you answer these 17 questions about three standout shortstops and their 1993 seasons? The answers to questions 1-12 are found in the 1993 Box Score Comparison on the next page. Ten correct answers makes you a major-leaguer; 12 vaults you to all-star status.

a. Ozzie Guillen
   Chicago White Sox

b. John Valentin
   Boston Red Sox

c. Ozzie Smith
   St. Louis Cardinals

1. Within what range did the trio's 1993 batting averages fall?

a. .265-.277
b. .278-.290
c. .291-.303

2. Who had the most at bats?

3. Who scored the most runs?

4. Who scored the fewest runs?

5. Who had the most hits?

6. Who had the most extra base hits (not including home runs)?

7. Who hit the most home runs?

8. Who hit the fewest home runs?

9. Who drove in the most runs?

10. Who stole the most bases?

11. Who stole the fewest bases?

12. Who committed the fewest errors?

EXTRA CREDIT
13. True or false: Ozzie Guillen's nickname is "The Wizard of Oz."

14. True or false: John Valentin is a product of the Boston Red Sox farm system.

15. True or false: Ozzie Smith began his major league career playing shortstop for the San Diego Padres.

16. True or false: Ozzie Smith never played in the minors.

17. True or false: Ozzie Guillen was Rookie of the Year in 1985.

1993 Box Score Comparison

Player	AVG	AB	R	H	XBH	HR	RBI	S	E
a. Ozzie Guillen	.280	453	44	127	27	4	5	50	16
b. John Valentin	.279	462	50	129	42	11	64	2	19
c. Ozzie Smith	.288	545	75	157	28	1	53	21	19

Answers to questions 13-17:

13. False, Ozzie Smith is nicknamed "The Wizard of Oz," not Ozzie Guillen.

14. True, before joining the Bosox in Fenway Park in Boston, John Valentin played shortstop for the Pawtucket at McCoy Stadium in Pawtucket, Rhode Island.

15. True, Ozzie Smith came up with the Padres in 1978. Four years later, San Diego and St. Louis exchanged shortstops; Ozzie Smith for Gary Templeton.

16. False, Ozzie Smith played about half-a-season of minor-league baseball before joining the major-league Padres as their everyday shortstop.

17. True, Ozzie Guillen (his given name is Oswaldo Jose Guillen Barrios) was Rookie of the Year in 1985. He led all American League shortstops in fielding percentage, committing a White Sox record low 12 errors, and batting .273. Guillen spent most of 1992 on the disabled list with a broken leg but played well in 1993, hitting .280.

DREAM TEAMS

Match the rosters below with the names and/or teams of these former MVPs. Make sure the name and team match the year he was the MVP. Twenty correct answers makes you a major-leaguer; 25 vaults you to all-star status.

AMERICAN LEAGUE

a. Eddie Collins, 1914

b. Zoilo Versalles, 1965

c. Dick Allen, 1972

d. Reggie Jackson, 1973

e. Thurman Munson, 1976

f. Don Baylor, 1979

g. George Brett, 1980

h. Willie Hernandez, 1984

i. George Bell, 1987

Player	**Position**	**Team**
1. _____	Pitcher	Detroit Tigers
2. _____	Catcher	_____
3. _____	First base	_____
4. _____	Second base	Philadelphia Athletics
5. _____	Third base	_____
6. _____	Shortstop	_____
7. _____	Outfield	_____
8. Jeff Burroughs, 1974	Outfield	_____
9. _____	Outfield	Oakland Athletics
10. _____	DH	_____

NATIONAL LEAGUE

a. Rogers Hornsby, 1925   d. Willie Mays, 1954   g. Mike Schmidt, 1980

b. Ernie Lombardi, 1938   e. Maury Wills, 1960   h. Dale Murphy 1982

c. Don Newcome, 1950   f. Willie Stargell, 1979

Player	Position	Team
1. _____	Pitcher	_____
2. _____	Catcher	Cincinnati Reds
3. _____	First base	_____
4. _____	Second base	St. Louis Cardinals
5. _____	Third base	_____
6. _____	Shortstop	_____
7. Andre Dawson, 1987	Outfield	_____
8. _____	Outfield	_____
9. _____	Outfield	Atlanta Braves

Answers: Dream Teams

AMERICAN LEAGUE

Player	Position	Team
1. Willie Hernandez	Pitcher	Detroit Tigers
2. Thurman Munson	Catcher	New York Yankees
3. Dick Allen	First base	Chicago White Sox
4. Eddie Collins	Second base	Philadelphia Athletics
5. George Brett	Third base	Kansas City Royals
6. Zoilo Versalles	Shortstop	Minnesota Twins
7. George Bell	Outfield	Toronto Blue Jays
8. Jeff Burroughs	Outfield	Texas Rangers
9. Reggie Jackson	Outfield	Oakland Athletics
10. Don Baylor	DH	California Angels

NATIONAL LEAGUE

Player	Position	Team
1. Don Newcome	Pitcher	Brooklyn Dodgers
2. Ernie Lombardi	Catcher	Cincinnati Reds
3. Willie Stargell	First base	Pittsburgh Pirates
4. Rogers Hornsby	Second base	St. Louis Cardinals
5. Mike Schmidt	Third base	Philadelphia Phillies
6. Maury Wills	Shortstop	Los Angeles Dodgers
7. Andre Dawson	Outfield	Chicago Cubs
8. Willie Mays	Outfield	New York Giants
9. Dale Murphy	Outfield	Atlanta Braves

WHO SAID IT? (PART II)

Can you identify who said what? Ten correct answers makes you a major-leaguer; 13 vaults you to all-star status.

a. Wade Boggs

b. Tim McCarver

c. Eddie Murray

d. Joe DiMaggio

e. Andy Van Slyke

f. George Bell

g. Billy Martin

h. Rusty Staub

i. Reggie Jackson

j. Satchel Paige

k. Mickey Mantle

l. Mitch Williams

m. Willie Mays

n. Dick Allen

o. Lenny Dykstra

1. A well-traveled former American league manager once said, "I have a confession to make. I have had pitchers who have thrown the spitball. My pitching coach, Art Fowler, has taught our pitchers (to throw it) ... and what's more, we have encouraged our pitchers to us it in a game."

_____

2. Mickey Rivers once said, "You got a white man's first name, a Puerto Rican's middle name and a black man's last name. No wonder you're so screwed up," to this Hall of Famer and New York Yankee teammate.

_____

3. Referring to former Texas Rangers Manager Bobby Valentine, this relief pitcher said, "He didn't like me I didn't like him, either. He tried to do what he does with everyone he doesn't

like – bury me." Instead of burying him, the Rangers traded him to the Chicago Cubs. In 1993, he was saving games for the pennant-winning Phillies, but was traded to Houston in 1994. Meanwhile, Valentine is managing the New York Mets' Triple A affiliate.

_____

4. Long-time pitcher Goose Gossage once described this person as "the best player I ever played with, in a league of his own ... nobody else is even close." The player so admired by Gossage was the 1964 Rookie of the Year with the Phillies and the 1972 MVP with the White Sox. Labelled "hard to handle," he moved from Philadelphia to St. Louis to Los Angeles to Chicago to Oakland, in that order, during his career. Lifetime, he hit .292 with 351 HRs and more than 1,100 RBI.

_____

5. In 1993, New York Mets Manager Dallas Green said this about his first baseman: "(He's) a veteran who does his own thing. I'm not wild about his preparation (for games), but he's not going to be with us next year." This person was released at the end of the 1993 and signed as a designated hitter in 1994 with the Cleveland Indians.

_____

6. This former Yankee superstar and husband of movie star Marilyn Monroe said, "Oh yes I have," when she bragged he had "never heard such applause" shortly after her return from a trip to Korea in 1954 to entertain U.S. troops.

_____

7. In 1993, this former New York/San Francisco Giant center fielder said, "I didn't think I could manage. I could have managed the Mets in 1975, but I said no ... it can be a thankless job." He was a .302 hitter with 660 HRs and 1,903 RBI. He also said, "He's still young and he's got a lot to learn," about his godson, Giant outfielder Barry Bonds.

_____

8. Barry Bonds once described this former teammate as the "Great White Hope." This Pittsburgh Pirate hit .310 with nine HRs and 50 RBI in 323 at bats during an injury-plagued 1993.

_____

9. Joe Carter, the Toronto Blue Jays' hero in the 1993 World Series, said "that little guy can flat out play" when describing this member of the Philadelphia Phillies. "That little guy," who also plays center field, hit .348, including four HRs, eight RBI and nine runs scored in the 1993 World Series.

_____

10. Former Yankee pitcher Ryne Duren once said this about his teammate: "When you lose a one-run game it kills you. (He) never helped you in the one-run games. He'd make the score 5-2 or 10-3." Lifetime, this person hit 536 HRs. Certainly some of those came in one-run games. He led the league in HRs four times, RBI once, batting average once and was an MVP three times.

_____

11. Early in the 1993 season, Yankee Owner George Steinbrenner had this to say about his new infielder's beard: "The way he hits, he can show up in his underwear."

_____

12. During his tenure as the New York Mets' manager, Joe Torre described this player by saying, "as a first baseman he's a great hitter." By 1993, this person had long been retired from playing the game but worked as a Met announcer and New York City restaurant owner.

_____

13. Chicago White Sox Manager Gene Lamont said this about his complaining designated hitter during the 1993 American League Championship Series: "The one thing (he) did is he bit the hand of one of his biggest backers, and maybe his most important backer."

_____

A 19-year-old Dwight Gooden struck out 276 batters and was named the National League Rookie of the Year in 1984. Gooden won the Cy Young Award in his second season, and was 119-46 after seven seasons.

14. This former major league catcher wrote about pitching in his book *Oh, Baby, I Love It*: "Three pitchers have dominated my big league playing and ... two are guys I caught in hundreds of games ... they are Bob Gibson and Steve Carlton. The third pitcher whom I have not had the good fortune to catch is Dwight Gooden, who seems irreversibly headed for the Hall of Fame."

_____

15. Joe DiMaggio, after a 1935 exhibition game, said "He's the best I've ever faced and the fastest." Too bad this pitcher didn't appear in the majors until he was 42 because of his race.

_____

Answers: *Who Said It? (Part II)*

1. g, Billy Martin also said, "I even managed against some (pitchers) who used the spitter when they pitched for me ... but you don't blow the whistle on them, even when they are pitching against you ... sort of honor among thieves."
2. i, Reginald Martinez Jackson
3. l, Mitch Williams
4. n, Dick Allen
5. c, Eddie Murray
6. d, Joe DiMaggio
7. m, Willie Mays
8. e, Andy Van Slyke
9. o, Lenny Dykstra
10. k, Mickey Mantle
11. a, Wade Boggs
12. h, Rusty Staub
13. f, George Bell was unhappy that he wasn't used by Manager Gene Lamont as a designated hitter against the Blue Jays in the ALCS. During the regular season that year, Bell hit .067 against Toronto.
14. b, Tim McCarver. As a 19-year-old rookie, Dwight Gooden struck out 276 batters and was named the National League Rookie of the Year in 1984. In his second season Gooden won the Cy Young Award. Through his first seven seasons Gooden was 119-46 (.721), the highest winning percentage in major-league history. Few would argue Gooden's road to Cooperstown will be a smooth one now that the bumps are behind him; bumps that included drinking and driving, fighting with police and 28 days of drug rehabilitation. Gooden was closest to the edge of disaster one night in December of 1986 when Tampa police pulled him over for weaving in and out of traffic. According to the Tampa police, Gooden, his 17-year-old nephew Gary Sheffield (now a star with the Florida Marlins) and three others were in Gooden's car. The police report stated the men were angry, argumentative and abusive when they approached the car. The police also claimed the men provoked a fistfight. Gooden's party claimed officers shouted "Break his arm," during the scuffle and another drew his pistol. Gooden, after pleading no contest to charges of resisting arrest and disorderly conduct, was placed on probation for three years.
15. j, As a major-league rookie well into his 40s, Satchel Paige helped the Cleveland Indians win the pennant in 1948. He compiled a 6-1 record with a 2.46 ERA that year. Though no one knows Paige's true age, he was believed to be between 42 and 48 years old in 1948, making him the oldest rookie in major league history.

1990s

Can you answer these multiple choice questions about baseball in the 1990s? Twelve correct answers makes you a major-leaguer; 15 vaults you to all-star status.

1. In 1991, Cecil Fielder became the first American Leaguer since 1970 to hit 40 or more home runs in consecutive seasons. Who equalled Fielder's feat in 1992-93?

a. Juan Gonzalez
b. Barry Bonds
c. Frank Thomas

2. Who leads all active players with 16 grand slam home runs?

a. Andres Galarraga
b. Don Mattingly
c. Eddie Murray

3. Which 1993 division-winner scored 877 runs, the most in 30 years?

a. Toronto
b. Chicago
c. Atlanta
d. Philadelphia

4. Which major-league team had four former Cy Young Award winners on its 1993 spring training roster?

a. New York Mets
b. Atlanta
c. Baltimore

5. Which New York Yankee pitcher became the first Australian to start a major league game as a rookie?

a. Mark Hutton
b. Bob Wickman
c. Sterling Hitchcock

6. At the conclusion of the 1992 season Ozzie Smith was awarded his 13th Gold Glove, breaking a tie with two others for the most Gold Gloves in National League history. Which of the following isn't a 12-time Gold Glove winner?

a. Ken Boyer
b. Willie Mays
c. Roberto Clemente

7. Two American Leaguers are their respective franchise's all-time leaders in singles, doubles, triples and home runs. Which of the following isn't a franchise leader?

a. Cal Ripken, Orioles
b. George Brett, Royals
c. Robin Yount, Brewers

8. Who, in 1993, tied the record of eight consecutive games with a home run?

a. Frank Thomas
b. Barry Bonds
c. Ken Griffey, Jr.

9. Who, in 1992, became the oldest player to drive in at least 100 RBI in a season?

a. Carlton Fisk
b. Dave Winfield
c. Eddie Murray

10. In 1992, Danny Tartabull became the second player in major league history to hit at least 25 home runs with three different teams before his 30th birthday. Who was the first?

a. Joe Carter
b. Dave Kingman
c. Ken Griffey

11. At 30 years old, Randy Smith became the youngest general manager in major league history when he took over what team?

a. 1990 Cincinnati Reds
b. 1992 Florida Marlins
c. 1993 San Diego Padres

12. Who set the American League rookie record of 66 stolen bases in 1992?

a. Scott Cooper
b. Pat Listach
c. Kenny Lofton

13. What New York pitcher allowed four runs while pitching a no-hitter in 1990?

a. Andy Hawkins, Yankees
b. Anthony Young, Mets
c. Melido Perez, Yankees

14. Bo Jackson gained notoriety for contributing in both professional football and major league baseball. What National Football League team did he play for?

a. Green Bay Packers
b. Pittsburgh Steelers
c. Los Angeles Raiders

15. What major league team did Bo Jackson play for before the Chicago White Sox?

a. Chicago Cubs
b. Kansas City Royals
c. California Angels

16. Who did Mike Ilitch, owner of the Little Caesar's Pizza franchise, purchase the Detroit Tigers from in 1992?

a. Bob and Rudy Carpenter
b. Domino's Pizza owner Tom Monaghan
c. Contractor Lou Perini

17. What pitcher led the league in strikeouts, pitched 200 or more innings and never missed a start from 1990-92?

a. Greg Maddux
b. Roger Clemens
c. David Cone

18. Florida Marlins pitcher Charlie Hough got his first hit of 1993 against the Expos. His last previous hit was exactly how many years earlier?

a. 5
b. 8
c. 13

Answers: 1990s

1. a, Juan Gonzalez
2. c, Eddie Murray
3. d, Philadelphia Phillies
4. b, Atlanta had Tom Glavine, Greg Maddux, Mark Davis and Steve Bedrosian attend spring training in 1993.
5. a, Mark Hutton
6. a, Ken Boyer
7. a, Cal Ripken
8. c, Ken Griffey, Jr.
9. b, Dave Winfield
10. b, Dave Kingman
11. c, 1993 San Diego Padres
12. c, Kenny Lofton
13. a, Andy Hawkins
14. c, Los Angeles Raiders
15. b, Kansas City Royals. Bo Jackson, the first athlete to play in the majors after recovering from hip replacement surgery, was a part-time designated hitter for the Chicago White Sox in 1993. The procedure forced Jackson to rely only on upper body strength when hitting and he ended the year with mediocre statistics. In his 281 at bats during the regular season, he hit 16 home runs (one every 17 at bats), but he also struck out 40 percent of the time while hitting only .232. Jackson and fellow Chicago designated hitter George Bell were critical of their manager, Gene Lamont, during the 1993 American League Championship Series against Toronto for being benched during Games 1 and 2. Perhaps Lamont knew what

he was doing, considering Jackson hit only .048 against the Blue Jays, and Bell just .065. Bell never played in the series. Jackson, however, played in the final three games, but was 0 for 10, including six strikeouts.

16. b, Tom Monaghan, owner of Domino's Pizza. Lou Perini purchased the Boston Braves in 1946 and five years later moved the team to Milwaukee. In the 1930s, the Philadelphia Phillies were owned by Gerry Nugent, who often sold his best players to other teams for cash. The practice caused the Phillies to perennially be near the bottom of the standings. In 1943 the National League stepped in and forced the sale of the club to William Cox. That same year, Cox was barred from baseball for betting on his team. In late 1943, Robert Carpenter, Jr. bought the team. He and his son, Rudy, ran the organization until 1982, when they sold it to Bill Giles and his group of investors.

17. c, David Cone
18. c, Charlie Hough went 13 years between hits. That's a long time, long enough for Hough to give up 2,354 hits (more than Joe DiMaggio had during his entire 13-year career). Hough was 45 years old in 1993, making him the oldest player in the majors. He was signed by the Florida Marlins in 1994, at a salary around $1 million for the season. Hough got the win in the expansion Marlins' first franchise victory in 1993.

HOME FIELD ADVANTAGE

Can you match the teams with their ballparks? Twenty-two correct answers makes you a major-leaguer; 30 vaults you to all-star status.

PRESENT AMERICAN LEAGUE BALLPARKS

a. The Ballpark

b. Metrodome

c. Municipal Stadium

d. Alameda Coliseum

e. Sky Dome

f. Comiskey Park

g. Kingdome

h. County Stadium

i. Camden Yards

j. Fenway Park

Team	Park
1. Toronto Blue Jays	_____
2. Baltimore Orioles	_____
3. Milwaukee Brewers	_____
4. Boston Red Sox	_____
5. Minnesota Twins	_____
6. Oakland Athletics	_____
7. Texas Rangers	_____
8. Chicago White Sox	_____
9. Kansas City Royals	_____
10. Seattle Mariners	_____

PRESENT NATIONAL LEAGUE BALLPARKS

a. Wrigley Field

b. Busch Stadium

c. Fulton County Stadium

d. Three River Stadium

e. Riverfront Stadium

f. Candlestick Park

g. Jack Murphy Stadium

h. Olympic Stadium

i. Shea Stadium

j. Astrodome

k. Mile High Stadium

l. Veteran's Memorial Stadium

m. Joe Robbie Stadium

Team	Park
1. Colorado Rockies	_____
2. Pittsburgh Pirates	_____
3. Montreal Expos	_____
4. St. Louis Cardinals	_____
5. New York Mets	_____
6. Chicago Cubs	_____
7. Philadelphia Phillies	_____
8. Florida Marlins	_____
9. Cincinnati Reds	_____
10. Atlanta Braves	_____
11. San Diego Padres	_____
12. San Francisco Giants	_____
13. Houston Astros	_____

PAST AMERICAN LEAGUE BALLPARKS

a. Memorial Stadium

b. Polo Grounds

c. Navin Field

d. Princeton Avenue Park

e. Exhibition Stadium

f. Wrigley Field

g. Huntington Avenue Ballpark

Team	Park
1. Boston Red Sox	_____
2. Toronto Blue Jays	_____
3. California Angels	_____
4. Baltimore Orioles	_____
5. Detroit Tigers	_____
6. New York Yankees	_____
7. Chicago White Sox	_____

PAST NATIONAL LEAGUE BALLPARKS

a. Polo Grounds

b. Jarry Park

c. Sportsmans' Park

d. Shibe Park

e. Seals Stadium

f. Forbes Field

g. Colt Stadium

Team	Park
1. Houston Astros	_____
2. Montreal Expos	_____
3. St. Louis Cardinals	_____
4. Pittsburgh Pirates	_____
5. New York Mets	_____
6. San Francisco Giants	_____
7. Philadelphia Phillies	_____

Answers: Home Field Advantage

PRESENT AMERICAN LEAGUE BALLPARKS

1. Toronto Blue Jays   e, Sky Dome
2. Baltimore Orioles   i, Camden Yards
3. Milwaukee Brewers   h, County Stadium
4. Boston Red Sox   j, Fenway Park
5. Minnesota Twins   b, Metrodome
6. Oakland Athletics   d, Alameda County
                             Coliseum
7. Texas Rangers   a, The Ballpark
8. Chicago White Sox   f, Comiskey Park
9. Kansas City Royals   c, Municipal
                             Stadium
10. Seattle Mariners   g, Kingdome

PRESENT NATIONAL LEAGUE BALLPARKS

1. Colorado Rockies   k, Mile High
                             Stadium
2. Pittsburgh Pirates   e, Three Rivers
                             Stadium
3. Montreal Expos   h, Olympic Stadium
4. St. Louis Cardinals   b, Busch Stadium
5. New York Mets   i, Shea Stadium
6. Chicago Cubs   a, Wrigley Field
7. Philadelphia Phillies l, Veterans Memorial
                             Stadium
8. Florida Marlins   m, Joe Robbie
                             Stadium
9. Cincinnati Reds   e, Riverfront
                             Stadium
10. Atlanta Braves   c, Fulton County
                             Stadium
11. San Diego Padres   g, Jack Murphy
                             Stadium
12. San Francisco Giants f, Candlestick Park
13. Houston Astros   j, Astrodome

PAST AMERICAN LEAGUE BALLPARKS

1. Boston Red Sox   g, Huntington
                             Avenue Ballpark
2. Toronto Blue Jays   e, Exhibition
                             Stadium
3. California Angels   f, Wrigley Field
4. Baltimore Orioles   a, Memorial Stadium
5. Detroit Tigers   c, Navin Field
6. New York Yankees   b, Polo Grounds
7. Chicago White Sox   d, Princeton Avenue
                             Ballpark

PAST NATIONAL LEAGUE BALLPARKS

1. Houston Astros   g, Colt Stadium
2. Montreal Expos   b, Jarry Park
3. St. Louis Cardinals   c, Sportsmans' Park
4. Pittsburgh Pirates   f, Forbes Field
5. New York Mets   a, Polo Grounds
6. San Francisco Giants   e, Seals' Stadium
7. Philadelphia Phillies d, Shibe Park

Selected Bibliography

Alexander, Charles C.
Our Game
New York, Henry Holt and Co., 1991

Astor, Gerand
The Baseball Hall of Fame 50th Anniversary
New Jersey, Prentice Hall Press, 1988

Cairns, Bob
Pen Men
New York, St. Martins Press, 1992

Connor, Anthony J.
Baseball For The Love Of It
New York, MacMillan Publishing Co., 1982

Dickey, Glen
The History of The World Series Since 1903
New York, Stein and Day, 1984

Golenbock, Peter
Dynasty, The New York Yankees 1949-64
New Jersey, Prentice-Hall Inc., 1975

Golenbock, Peter
Fenway
New York, G.P. Putnam's Sons, 1992

Gutman, Dan
Baseball Babylon
U.S.A., Penguin Books, 1992

Hough, John Jr.
A Player For The Moment
New York, Harcourt Brace Jovanovich, 1988

Nemec, David
Greenbecker, Matthew D.
Schlossberg, Dan
Johnson, Dick
Tully, Mike
Players of Cooperstown
Lincolnwood Illinois
Publications International Ltd., 1993
Nettles, Graig with Golenbock, Peter Balls
New York, G.P. Putnam's Sons, 1984

Pascarelli, Peter
The Toughest Job in Baseball
New York, Simon and Schuster, 1993

Reichler, Joseph L., Editor
The World Series, A 75th Anniversary
New York, Simon and Schuster, 1978

Reichler, Joseph L., Editor
The Baseball Encyclopedia
New York, MacMillan Publishing, 1988

Rogosin, Donn
Invisible Men
New York, Atheneum, 1983

Ryan, Nolan with Herskowitz, Mickey
Kings Of The Hill
U.S.A., Harper Collins, 1992

Schoor, Gene
The History Of The World Series
New York, William Morrow and Co., 1990

Selected Bibliography

Shatzkin, Mike, Editor with Charlton, Jim
The Ballplayers
New York, Arbor House/William Morrow,
1990

Siwoff, Seymour S. with Hirdt, Steve, Tom and Peter
The Elias Baseball Analyst
New York, Simon and Schuster, 1992

Smith, Robert
Pioneers in Baseball
U.S.A., Little Brown and Co., 1978

Sugar, Bert R., Editor
Baseballistics
New York, St. Martins Press, 1990

Thorn, John
A Century of Baseball
NYC, Hart Publishing Co., 1974

Waggoner, Glen and Moloney, Kathleen and Howard, Hugh
Baseball By The Rules
U.S.A., Taylor Publishing Co., 1987

Wilbur, Cynthia J.
For The Love Of The Game
New York, William Morrow & Co., 1992

Zoss, Joel and Bowman, John
Diamonds In The Rough
New York, MacMillan Publishing, 1989

Get into the game!

Masters Press has a complete line of books to help
coaches and participants alike "master their game."

All of our books are available at better bookstores or by calling Masters Press
at 1-800-722-2677, or 317-298-5706. Catalogs are available upon request.

Our other puzzle books include the following:

Baseball Crosswords

By Mark Roszkowski

A fun new way for baseball fans of all ages to enjoy their favorite sport! Each chapter includes a condensed history of a major league team, a crossword puzzle full of names from the team's past and present, a summary of 1993 team leaders, a graph of the team's finishes over the last ten years and a list of league leaders from each team during that period.

$12.95 ● paper ● 160 pages ● puzzles and graphs
ISBN 0-940279-55-X

Basketball Crosswords

By Dale Ratermann

If you love professional basketball, this is the book for you! A complete collection of crosswords based solely on the NBA. The book includes a chapter on each of the 27 NBA teams with a team history, key statistics, and a crossword puzzle with clues to test your knowledge of NBA history and players.

$12.95 ● paper ● 192 pages ● photos and puzzles
ISBN 0-940279-75-4

Football Crosswords

By Dale Ratermann

Enjoy football in a whole new way with our unique collection of football crosswords. Chapters are devoted to each of the NFL's 28 teams prior to the 1994 expansion. They include a brief team history, a crossword puzzle devoted exclusively to that team, and relevant statistical information.

$12.95 ● paper ● 192 pages ● photos and puzzles
ISBN 0-940279-74-6

MASTERS PRESS

DEAR VALUED CUSTOMER,

Masters Press is dedicated to bringing you timely and authoritative books for your personal and professional library. As a leading publisher of sports and fitness books, our goal is to provide you with easily accessible information on topics that interest you written by the most qualified authors. You can assist us in this endeavor by checking the box next to your particular areas of interest.

We appreciate your comments and will use the information to provide you with an expanded and more comprehensive selection of titles.

Thank you very much for taking the time to provide us with this helpful information.

Cordially,
Masters Press

Areas of interest in which you'd like to see Masters Press publish books:

☐ COACHING BOOKS
   Which sports? What level of competition?

☐ INSTRUCTIONAL/DRILL BOOKS
   Which sports? What level of competition?

☐ FITNESS/EXERCISE BOOKS
   ☐ Strength—Weight Training
   ☐ Body Building
   ☐ Other

☐ REFERENCE BOOKS
   what kinds?

☐ BOOKS ON OTHER
   Games, Hobbies or Activities

Are you more likely to read a book or watch a video-tape to get the sports information you are looking for?

I'm interested in the following sports as a participant:

I'm interested in the following sports as an observer:

Please feel free to offer any comments or suggestions to help us shape our publishing plan for the future.

Name _____ Age _____

Address _____

City _____ State _____ Zip _____

Daytime phone number _____

BUSINESS REPLY MAIL

FIRST CLASS MAIL   PERMIT NO. 1317   INDIANAPOLIS IN

POSTAGE WILL BE PAID BY ADDRESSEE

MASTERS PRESS

2647 WATERFRONT PKY EAST DR
INDIANAPOLIS IN 46209-1418

NO POSTAGE
NECESSARY
IF MAILED
IN THE
UNITED STATES